BEYOND
ANSWERS

Mike Flynn

BEYOND ANSWERS

Exploring
MATHEMATICAL PRACTICES
with Young Children

Foreword by Deborah Schifter

Stenhouse
PUBLISHERS

www.stenhouse.com

Library of Congress Cataloging-in-Publication Data

Names: Flynn, Michael, 1974-
Title: Beyond answers : exploring mathematical practices with young children
  / Michael Flynn.
Description: Portland, Maine. : Stenhouse Publishers, 2016. | Includes
  bibliographical references and index.
Identifiers: LCCN 2016021338 (print) | LCCN 2016037355 (ebook) | ISBN
  9781571109026 (pbk. : alk. paper) | ISBN 9781625311474 (ebook)
Subjects: LCSH: Communication in mathematics. | Mathematics--Study and
  teaching (Early childhood) | Reasoning in children. | Education--Parent participation.
Classification: LCC QA41.4 .F59 2016 (print) | LCC QA41.4 (ebook) | DDC
  372.7/049--dc23
LC record available at https://lccn.loc.gov/2016021338

Cover and interior design by Lucian Burg, LU Design Studios, Portland, ME

Manufactured in the United States of America

PRINTED ON 30% PCW
RECYCLED PAPER

23 22 21 20 19   9 8 7 6 5 4 3 2

Dedicated to Megan, Dan, Allison, Sean, and Collin

for all their love and support

CONTENTS

FOREWORD

Whether or not individual states decide to adopt it, the Common Core State Standards have provided a gift in the list of Standards for Mathematical Practice. The eight standards identify behaviors, or practices, that students enact in order to understand and become proficient in mathematics:

1. Make sense of problems and persevere in solving them.
2. Reason abstractly and quantitatively.
3. Construct viable arguments and critique the reasoning of others.
4. Model with mathematics.
5. Use appropriate tools strategically.
6. Attend to precision.
7. Look for and make use of structure.
8. Look for and express regularity in repeated reasoning.

With the guidance of this list, teachers can move toward a teaching practice that instills in their students an appreciation of mathematics as a realm of interconnected concepts to be explored, understood, and exploited to solve a wide range of problems. Indeed, professional mathematicians employ these same practices when they create new mathematics.

One might ask, Is it reasonable to expect young children, near the beginning of their lives as mathematical thinkers, to enact the practices of mathematicians at the top of their field? The answer is a resounding "yes"! As Mike Flynn illustrates in this book, five-, six-, seven-, and eight-year-olds can and do behave like mathematicians.

Though the Common Core document dedicates a paragraph to each of the practice standards, the language may be difficult for many teachers to interpret. What does it mean to reason quantitatively or to make use of structure? What is a viable argument in primary grades? What is a mathematical model? Flynn, a former second-grade teacher who worked with colleagues to make sense of the standards, explains in simple language.

Each chapter of this book is dedicated to a different practice and begins with a story from Flynn's life outside of school to portray the practice's essence. Then, staying close to the text of the Common Core, Flynn digs in to each practice and discusses its different components. Using vivid examples from actual classrooms, he shows how the practice is enacted at different levels, from kindergarten to second grade. The reader has access not only to the words, actions, and writing of young children, but also to the teacher's thinking as he or she sets up the task, interacts with students, and reflects on the lesson afterward. Prior to each vignette, Flynn poses focus questions to guide the reader's attention; following each vignette, he elaborates on strategies for implementation.

This book is for primary-grade teachers to read solo or as a group. Using the many examples and suggestions, teachers will be well positioned to try activities with their students. They will be on the lookout for ideas that are likely to arise in their classrooms and will have new strategies to address them. Teachers reading the book together will have opportunities to discuss vignettes, make action plans, and compare the results of the strategies they implement.

This book is for other educators—mathematics methods teachers or professional development staff—who are responsible for helping primary-grade teachers understand the Standards for Mathematical Practice.

This book is for parents who want to better understand the mathematical thinking of their young children. The many illustrations of children's mathematical ideas are likely to spark explorations at home.

Anyone curious about children's mathematical creativity and the potential for math exploration in the classroom will enjoy reading this accessible book.

Deborah Schifter
Education Development Center,
Waltham, Massachusetts

ACKNOWLEDGMENTS

First and foremost I would like to thank my wife, Megan, for her continuous encouragement and support throughout the whole writing process. She is an amazing thought partner and challenged me to dig deeper and reach higher with this work.

I want to thank my children, Dan, Allison, Sean, and Collin, for their love, support, and patience. Their own mathematical development taught me so much about how young children make sense of mathematical ideas, and they continue to impress me as I watch them grow and develop into strong thinkers.

Special thanks to my editor, Toby Gordon, who believed in me and helped me shape the plan for this book. Her endless patience and support were greatly appreciated as I worked over the years to finish the manuscript. I could not have asked for a better, more encouraging editor. Thank you, Toby!

I must also thank another Stenhouse editor and author, Tracy Zager, for her support during this process. Our weekly productivity check-ins kept me focused on writing and provided much-needed motivation to get this manuscript finished.

Thanks as well to all the other folks at Stenhouse who helped make this book possible: Dan Tobin, Chandra Lowe, Chris Downey, Jay Kilburn, and Louisa Irele. It has been an exciting process to put this book together, and I am very thankful for all you have done to help make it happen.

I would not be in the position to write a math book if it weren't for my friend, colleague, and mentor Anne Marie O'Reilly, who supported me in my first years of teaching and introduced me to the world of professional learning in mathematics. Anne Marie's guidance shaped my entire career pathway in mathematics, and I will forever be grateful for her support.

I would also like to thank my former principal, Bill Collins. His support of my approach to teaching afforded me the autonomy I needed to be successful in the classroom. He trusted my judgment and supported the many projects in which I was involved. He was an incredible school leader, mentor, and friend.

Deborah Schifter, Virginia Bastable, Susan Jo Russell, and Myriam Steinback were integral to deepening my own understanding of mathematics and my knowledge of how students think and learn. I am grateful to have been a part of their many projects in math education over the years. These were powerful professional learning experiences, and they connected me with many talented and brilliant educators and mathematicians from across the country. I also want to thank Deborah for her guidance and support as she read numerous drafts of the manuscript and provided essential feedback throughout the process. I am honored that she wrote the foreword for the book and appreciate all she has done to help make *Beyond Answers* what it is.

I have a number of colleagues from different schools and organizations who have influenced my teaching over the years, and I would like to recognize them. They include my former colleagues at the William E. Norris Elementary School, TERC Investigations authors and my fellow workshop leaders, facilitators from Mathematics Leadership Programs at Mount Holyoke College, the Professional Development Student Group, educators in the Math/Twitter/Blogosphere commonly known as #MTBoS, the Teachers Development Group, and the various teachers I encountered over the years through projects and professional learning experiences.

Writing this book—which includes pseudonyms for all teachers' and students' names—would not have been possible if it hadn't been for all the teachers who opened their classrooms to me, shared vignettes, provided student work samples, engaged in conversations, challenged my thinking, and submitted written contributions. Their collective work contributed to and inspired the classroom vignettes in this book. Those teachers are Sarah Bent, Jessica Boland, Dayle Bowler, Katy Brunelle, Jayne Byrne, Laure Frye, Jim Hanson, Jennifer Hawkins, Cheryl Heldt, Katie Hurckes, Courtney Keegan, Mary Keller, Lauren Lamb, Sara McGee, Susan Miller, Nonye Obiora, Anne Marie O'Reilly, Lisa Peloquin, Jessica Reed, Karen Schweitzer, Britney Skiff, Stephanie Sluyter, Rita Smith, Amany Soliman, Judy Stearns, Kaneka Turner, Kristen Valenti, Chaya Venkatesh, LeeAnn Wells, Michael Wilson, Ann Zito, and Eileen Zymroz.

Finally, I would like to thank all my former second graders. For fourteen years, I had the honor and privilege of exploring mathematical ideas with these seven- and eight-year-olds. They pushed my thinking and challenged my conception of the capabilities of second graders. Our days were full of discoveries, new insights, and productive struggles. My work with these students greatly influenced my whole approach to math education. I will always look back fondly on our work together.

INTRODUCTION

Lost in Boston: A Case for Meaningful Math Instruction

Early in my driving career I developed a bit of an aversion to city driving, thanks to a few unpleasant experiences trying to navigate my way around Boston. If you've never had the pleasure of driving there, you should know that Boston has nothing like the pristine grid system of a well-designed city. It's a maze of narrow, winding streets that were laid out during colonial times. On top of that, constant road construction and detours can make even the most seasoned traveler feel a bit shell-shocked. So anytime I had to go to Boston, I would do my best to avoid driving.

This avoidance strategy worked well until 2008, when I had to travel to the city almost weekly to attend meetings and conferences. My first few trips were disastrous to say the least. I downloaded the directions from Google Maps and reviewed them many times to commit the steps to memory. Things went fairly well until I got into the city, where I always seemed to miss a turn at some point. Once that happened, panic set in as I became utterly lost. After a frantic few minutes of randomly driving around, I realized I had only two options: double back and retrace my steps in hopes of finding the correct turn or pull off and ask someone for directions.

These strategies usually worked and I would eventually arrive fashionably late for my meetings. However, on one trip, even those solutions did not help. While trying in vain to find a specific hotel, I stopped at a gas station and showed the guy behind the counter my directions in hopes of getting some assistance. He just laughed at me and said, "You'll never find it. Two of the roads on your directions don't even exist anymore." After that, I began leaving thirty to forty minutes earlier just to give myself a little "getting lost" time.

Then one afternoon as I was making the two-hour drive home, reflecting on how much I hated to drive in the city, I had an epiphany. Driving in Boston felt a lot like how learning math felt when I was a student. The directions seemed simple enough, but inevitably things would go wrong and I would be left driving around aimlessly, trying to find a familiar sight to help me get back on track. Even though people helped me, I was still at the mercy of their directions. This same level of discomfort, vague understanding, and reliance on others is exactly what I experienced as a student in math class.

Growing up, I learned math in a very traditional manner. Basically, math instruction consisted of learning various procedures for solving problems, followed by lots of practice toward mastering the steps. I rarely had opportunities to understand the mathematics behind the procedures, because, according to my teachers, if I remembered the steps, I would solve the problems correctly. They even had little tricks to help us remember the steps. One classic trick was "Yours is not to reason why, just invert and multiply."

On the surface, this seemed simple enough. However, I didn't always remember the steps, or I would make a mistake with one of them, particularly if the problems were put into different contexts. Was I supposed to invert the first fraction or the second? Or was it both? Did I multiply across or diagonally? When this happened, I was lost in the problem and had two choices: retrace my steps or raise my hand and ask for help. Sound familiar?

In Boston, I had no sense of the area. Street names were meaningless, and landmarks were simply random points of interest. In math, I had no conceptual understanding of the underlying procedures. I knew the steps, but they had no meaning for me. In both cases, I was simply relying on memory to reach my goal. If things went well and I did not run into snags like detours or a missed step, I found my destination or got the right answer. More often than not, I had to appeal for help. And even when I did reach my destination, I really didn't understand how I arrived there.

So how did I deal with the Boston issue? Clearly, I could not rely on my forty-minute "getting lost" buffer as a solution. Not only was it inefficient, but I also ran the risk of being late for events and important meetings. I know what you're thinking—and I did purchase a GPS navigation device. The problem was that it would often lose satellite contact once I entered a tunnel, and take five minutes to reset. When it stopped working, I was worse off than before, because I did not print out directions. Also, the GPS device doesn't help you learn how to navigate. It just tells you where to go. What I needed to do was learn Boston.

First, I contacted my brother, who used to own and operate a limousine company and whose clients required travel to and from Boston. An expert on navigating the city, he was an ideal person to help me. In exchange for lunch and dinner (his choice), he agreed to ride with me to Boston. In preparation for the trip, he had me identify the major arteries and helped me recognize key landmarks and how to use them as points of reference. We then packed our map and hit the road.

Once in the city, Scott had me pull over so we could locate our position on the map. He then had me find a destination on the map and chart a course. As I drove, he reminded me to find the key landmarks to help keep my bearings and asked guiding questions such as "What turn do you need to make next?" or "If you are planning to get on Beacon Street, which lane should you be in?" Even when he could see I was going to make a mistake, he never told me what to do. Instead, he would let me miss the turn and ask me to think about what I had done wrong. At first this was exceedingly frustrating because it meant I had to get us back to where I had made the mistake, but then I saw how helpful his strategy was.

Think about it. Instead of simply telling me to get in the right lane, he would ask me what I needed to do. This required me to think about my current location, my destination, and what I needed to do next. It was not a big deal when I made a mistake because I was able to learn more of Boston as I found my way back and then learn from my mistake. All decisions had to come from me, which meant I was developing an understanding of the area rather than following directions. In a short time, I became quite familiar with Boston and developed some successful strategies for driving around in the city. By the end of the day, I knew the area well enough to navigate it without specific directions and was confident in my abilities to get anywhere using multiple routes.

Sure, this was an extreme measure to take to learn how to navigate an area. However, it was well worth it because I now understood an area I would have to visit once or twice a week for much of the year.

Why am I telling you all this? Simply put, I think we need to approach math instruction more like the way I learned Boston—through purposeful, guided exploration. This means giving students time to learn any particular mathematical concept through a variety of experiences with support from the teacher. If students get lost, we support them to find out what went wrong and what they can do to avoid similar issues in the future. Consider the case from Joanne's first-grade classroom in which a student continues to make the same error but does not recognize it.

Joanne's first-grade students were working on addition problems and encouraged to use strategies that made sense to them. Some students used interlocking cubes to model the problems, others drew pictures, and one girl, Alicia, was using a number line. When Joanne observed Alicia working, she noticed each of her answers was one less than the correct answer. She was fairly certain she knew why Alicia was making that mistake and sat down to chat with her.

Joanne: I noticed you decided to use the number line today. How is it working for you?

Alicia: Good. I didn't want to use cubes.

Joanne: That's great. I think you are the first student this year to try the number line. Can you show me how you're using it with the next problem?

> || **JOEY AND KYLIE WERE COUNTING ANIMALS IN THE PARK. JOEY COUNTED 13 CATS AND KYLIE COUNTED 9 DOGS. HOW MANY ANIMALS DID THEY COUNT ALTOGETHER?**

Alicia: Okay, I start by finding the first number. (She puts her pencil over 13 on the number line.) Then I count up 9. (She begins counting on the 13 and continues until she gets to 21.) And then it's 21 so I write it down.

First graders often make this mistake when using a number line to solve problems. Instead of starting their counting on the number after the first addend, they start counting on the first addend. Joanne easily could have pointed out the error to Alicia, but instead engaged in a conversation to help Alicia recognize the error and solution for herself.

Joanne: I see some really good thinking here. Do you remember how we talked about checking your work using another strategy? (Alicia nods.) What strategy do you want to use to check this last problem?

Alicia: (Pause.) I could use pictures.

Joanne: Great. Let's see how that works.

Alicia begins by writing the number 13 on her paper and circling it. Although it's not said here, this is her way of showing that she put 13 in her head. She then draws 9 circles next to it. When she is finished, she says 13 aloud and then counts on, using the circles, and gets 22 for an answer. She looks a little unsure, so she counts them again to confirm her answer.

Alicia: So it's 22 and not 21.

Joanne: What makes you say that?

Alicia: Because I counted it two times.

Joanne: Why do you think you got 21 using the number line? (Alicia shrugs.) Let's try using the number line to solve a very small problem and see if it helps us think about what's happening on the number line. Try solving 2 plus 2 on the number line.

Alicia laughs as she prepares to solve 2 plus 2. She begins with her pencil on 2 and says, "One, two" as she points to the 2 and the 3. Alicia recognizes the mistake and quickly goes back and repeats the steps, but this time begins counting on the 3 and ends up with 4 as her answer.

Joanne: What happened?

Alicia: I counted it wrong. You don't count the number you're on. You have to start here. (She points to the 3.)

Joanne: How do you know?

Alicia: Because I got 3 and I know it's wrong.

Joanne: So you start counting from the number next to your starting number? (Alicia nods.) Can we try using the number line again to solve that last problem?

Alicia successfully uses the number line with the 13 + 9 problem and also notes that she has to go back and fix all her other answers. Before finishing, Joanne wants to help Alicia make one more connection.

Joanne: Before you fix your other problems, I want you to see something. Let's look back at how you solved this problem with pictures. What did you do?

Alicia: I put 13 in my head and then counted up 9 more.

Joanne: When you counted the first circle, did you count it as 13 or 14?

Alicia: Fourteen.

Joanne: And why was it 14 and not 13?

Alicia: Because the 13 was already here. (She points to the 13, and then pauses while thinking.) Oh! I get it. That's why I had to start counting here. (She points to the 14 on the number line.)

In this instance, Joanne saw her student becoming lost when she tried using a new strategy. On the surface this seems like an easy fix: just tell her to start counting on the number after the first addend. However, Joanne recognized the complexity of the number line when first graders begin using it and decided to allow Alicia to play around with it so she could discover her own error and understand what went wrong. Joanne helped facilitate this discovery by asking very purposeful questions that required Alicia to focus on how she was counting. In doing so, Alicia was able to make sense of counting on the number line on her own and learn the importance of checking one's work.

Our main goal as math teachers is not to help our students *do* math, but to help our students *understand* math. If we focus our attention on understanding, then students will develop a level of efficiency and accuracy that goes beyond what those of us from traditional backgrounds were able to accomplish. Consider how well you know your hometown. Your intimate knowledge of the area allows you to get from Point A to Point B in a variety of ways, using your experience, knowledge of short-cuts, and understanding of traffic patterns. We want our students to develop the same familiarity with mathematics. We want math to become their neighborhood.

Imagine that Massachusetts has changed its rules for issuing drivers' licenses. They now require all applicants to take another driving exam that involves driving from one's hometown to various destinations throughout the state within a certain amount of time. Naturally, drivers in the western part of the state are expected to get to multiple destinations in and around Boston. Accuracy is important as well as flexibility and adaptability. This new exam would have a significant effect on drivers' education courses and require instructors to help students prepare for it. Now imagine that you are charged with designing a one-week course for students preparing to take the exam. What does that course look like? What experiences do you want the students to have? What knowledge and skills do they need?

When I teach courses or lead seminars on teaching mathematics, I often present the same scenario to the participants. Surprisingly, regardless of geographic location, they all describe similar ideas: students should know how to follow directions and have an understanding of road maps, they should know how to navigate detours and use technology (GPS), and they should have a general sense of the area to which they are traveling. Most importantly, every group says they would spend the bulk of their week with students actually driving around in Boston. As one participant in New Mexico said, "The best way to learn an area is to explore it."

It makes sense. If people spent time navigating Boston, they would eventually get a sense of the area and be able to find various destinations regardless of detours, missed turns, and so forth. Additionally, they would most likely find routes that are faster than those suggested by sites such as Google Maps. Of course, the initial driving would be inefficient, with students making mistakes and getting confused, but with guidance, they would develop an intuitive sense of their surroundings and truly know the area.

Holding On to the Past

Whenever I present this scenario of a fictitious driving test to teachers, they all agree students need to develop a deep understanding of the area so they can learn multiple ways to reach the same destination. Yet, many of these teachers also tell me kids need to be shown how to solve problems in math. What is their rationale behind this assertion? Some say it is how they learned and it worked for them. Others say it is the only approach they know. Although I have a different view of mathematics instruction, I do understand their point of view, because I once shared it.

We can teach only what we know, and since many of us in the profession have come from a traditional background in math instruction, it is only natural that we gravitate toward the same approach. However, just because that was what we experienced, that doesn't mean it is the best approach.

Think about what going to the dentist was like when you were younger. I have vivid memories of terrible-tasting chemicals in my mouth, the painful drill they used that actually caused smoke to come out of my mouth, and the soreness once the Novocain wore off. It was an excruciating experience that I would not wish upon anyone. Today, they have drills that are smaller and faster, and some have lasers on the end that gently numb the area, eliminating the need for Novocain in some cases. Can you imagine adults insisting that their dentists use the old equipment on their children because that was what worked for them? It sounds preposterous, but that is exactly what happens with math. Education, just like all other professions, evolves as researchers and practitioners gain more insights into what works and what doesn't.

When I ask primary-grade teachers how they feel about math, many express a dislike for the subject. When I press them further about why they don't like math, they usually refer to their own experiences as students. They recall having to stand up at the board and solve problems in front of their peers, completing countless piles of worksheets, being subjected to high-pressure timed tests of basic facts, and lacking any strong understanding of the material. Like me, they understood enough of the basics, but once they encountered more complex mathematics, such as high school algebra, things started to fall apart because we never developed a strong conceptual understanding.

Until we break this cycle of teaching math procedurally, we are going to continue to struggle as a country with the subject. When I became a teacher and found that showing students how to solve math problems was not working, I realized I needed to change my approach to teaching mathematical content. It was then that I began my journey toward teaching math for understanding.

A New Approach

Math reform is not a new concept. In fact, since the sixties the pendulum has swung between reform and a "back to the basics" approach. More recent reform efforts include the work of the National Council of Teachers of Mathematics (NCTM) highlighted in *Principles and Standards for School Mathematics* (2000) and further clarified in *Curriculum Focal Points* (2006). These two critical movements helped inform the development of the Common Core State Standards for Mathematics (McCallum 2015). The essential premise behind all of these efforts is to encourage and support math instruction that develops conceptual understanding with procedural proficiency. In other words, we want our students to engage in mathematical tasks efficiently, accurately, and with conceptual understanding (Boaler, Williams, and Confer 2015). We want math to make sense to our students, and for our students to make sense of math.

We need to give students the opportunity to develop their own rich and deep understanding of our number system. With that understanding, they will be able to develop and use a wide array of strategies in ways that make sense for the problem at hand. It means slowing down and giving students lots of experience exploring various mathematical concepts (McCallum 2015). Accomplishing this change of approach toward math instruction often requires a major shift in the role of the teacher.

It is not easy, but we need to shift from being the givers of knowledge to becoming the facilitators of knowledge development. My biggest fear when I made the transition was that I would lose control of the lessons, the math, and the class. The thought of allowing students to solve problems in different ways was unnerving in the beginning. What if I did not understand what they were doing? What if their strategy took forever to complete? How would I get everyone to the same level of understanding?

Again, consider the driving scenario and imagine riding in the passenger seat as your student is about to make a wrong turn. You know this mistake will take you on a long detour, and you'll have to navigate many one-way streets to get back to the correct turn. You can easily avoid this headache if you simply tell the student the correct turn. The temptation is great, and with just that little hint, you will arrive at your destination. However, will the driver internalize the reason for making that turn, or know it only because you told her?

Let's explore this same idea

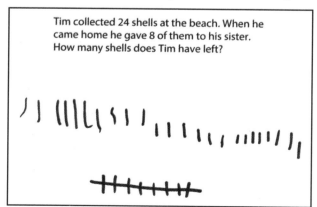

Tim collected 24 shells at the beach. When he came home he gave 8 of them to his sister. How many shells does Tim have left?

Figure 1 Aiden's work

but from a classroom perspective. While introducing subtraction story problems to my second graders, Aiden, one of my students, was having difficulty with the work. When I sat down with Aiden, I first looked at his work to get a sense of his approach to the problem (see Figure 1).

I could see that he had drawn 24 tally marks and 8 tally marks. Then he crossed out the 8, but he was stuck on what to do next. If this had occurred during my first years of teaching, I would have simply told him it was a subtraction problem and he needed to draw only 24 marks. I would have then told him to cross out 8 and count the leftovers. He would have gotten the correct answer, but only because he complied with what I asked him to do. Instead, I engaged in the following discussion with him.

Me: What's the problem, Aiden?

Aiden: I know it's take-away, but I don't think I'm doing it right.

Me: How do you know it's take-away?

Aiden: Because he's giving some of his shells away.

Me: How many shells did Tim start with?

Aiden: Twenty-four.

Me: Do you think your answer will be greater or less than 24?

Aiden: Less.

Me: Why?

Aiden: Because he's giving some away.

At this point I was fairly confident Aiden had an understanding of subtraction as removal or "take-away." His difficulty seemed to be with the approach to solving a subtraction problem rather than the concept of subtraction. I continued to engage in conversation with him.

Me: Tell me about your strategy. How are you trying to solve this?

Aiden: Well, I drew 24 marks and then drew 8 marks, but I don't know what to do next because if I take 8 away, I keep getting 24.

Me: Okay, tell me why you drew 24 tally marks. What do they represent? (He furrows his brow, so I rephrase.) What do they stand for in the problem?

Aiden: The shells Tim had at the beach.

Me: And what did he do with some of his shells?

Aiden: He gave 8 to his sister.

Me: How could you show that with your picture?

Aiden: Right here (points to the 8 extra tallies).

Me: But if these (pointing to the 24 tallies) are the shells Tim starts with, what are these?

Aiden: The ones he gives away.

Me: If you have those 8 as well, how many tallies are there altogether?

Aiden: (Counts them.) Thirty-two. That's too many.

Me: Right, so where do the 8 he gives away have to come from?

Aiden: Oh. From these (points to the 24).

Me: How could you do that?

Aiden: I can cross out 8 from here.

Aiden proceeded to erase the extra 8 he drew and then crossed out 8 from the original 24. He then counted the leftovers and wrote his answer: 16. With a look of satisfaction on his face, he eagerly began the next problem.

My interaction with Aiden took longer than it would have if I had simply told him what to do, but the exchange was much more effective in helping him discover his error and learn to solve subtraction problems in ways that made sense to him. Some questions to consider:

- What was my role in this exchange?
- How did this exchange help Aiden move beyond his difficulty?
- What might be some next steps for Aiden?

Because I focused my efforts on questioning rather than telling Aiden what to do, the problem solving had to come from him. Although I knew what his mistake was, I wanted him to discover it. As a result, he learned why his original strategy was giving him difficulty and had a better sense of how to approach these problems in the future. Additionally, we discussed this problem and Aiden's discovery with the whole class at the end of the lesson. This helped him deepen his understanding of his new discovery and share his ideas for the benefit of the class.

This shift from teacher-led instruction focused on procedures to student-centered learning focused on developing conceptual understandings is a major component of the Common Core State Standards for Mathematics; central to this work are the standards for Mathematical Practice. The eight standards are as follows:

1. Make sense of problems and persevere in solving them.
2. Reason abstractly and quantitatively.
3. Construct viable arguments and critique the reasoning of others.
4. Model with mathematics.
5. Use appropriate tools strategically.

6. Attend to precision.
7. Look for and make use of structure.
8. Look for and express regularity in repeated reasoning.

These practices describe the ways in which mathematically proficient students engage with mathematics on a daily basis. For each practice standard, accompanying text describes what this work looks like in K–12 classrooms. The problem with the descriptions is that they cover a wide range of grades in just a few short paragraphs. As a result, it can be difficult for primary-grade teachers to get a sense of what these practices look like with kindergartners and first and second graders.

This book aims to clarify the Standards for Mathematical Practice in the primary grades and give concrete examples in the form of vignettes to support K–2 teachers in their efforts to implement the practices in their classrooms. The Standards for Mathematical Practice require a significant cognitive demand on the part of students as they progress through the grades. For students to truly engage in these practices, the math work needs to be more student centered and less teacher directed.

Although this book is focused primarily on the Standards for Mathematical Practice, we will explore a lot of math content and pedagogical moves that support this work. You may find that some of these ideas are new to you. I suggest you note these areas so you can begin to create your own professional learning plan.

Many of the teachers featured in this book use the Investigations in Number, Data, and Space series (TERC 2016). Vignettes from their classrooms highlight activities and tasks from the Investigations program or adaptations of those activities. It is important to note that the Standards for Mathematical Practice are not program specific. Your students will have opportunities to engage in this work regardless of the curriculum series you use.

As you read, keep the context of driving in Boston in the back of your mind. The difference between someone telling you how to get somewhere and learning the area for yourself is significant. The former, although quick and simple, provides one with a limited understanding. The latter requires more time and effort, but results in a more comprehensive understanding and allows one to truly know the area. As you consider your students, which approach do you want to take with them during your math class?

CHAPTER 1

Mathematical Practice 1: Make Sense of Problems and Persevere in Solving Them

This past winter, my rambunctious golden retriever, Lucy, excitedly jumped up on the old wooden storm door of my front porch to greet and bark at the mailman. This was a favorite habit of hers, much to the shock and annoyance of our neighborhood letter carrier. On this particular day, Lucy managed to crack the wooden frame of the door, rendering it useless and requiring me to buy and install a new door during the frigid month of January.

If you've never had the privilege of installing a storm door, consider yourself lucky. It involves a lot of finesse to ensure a square fit, and you must address many slight variables of your individual house. In my case, the railings on the front steps required that the door open inward. To accomplish this, I had to reverse all of the directions provided in the already complicated instruction manual. Oh, and did I mention I am not handy?

After about an hour of trying to get my head around how to make this work, I decided to throw in the towel and call a fix-it man to install the door. He told me he would charge eighty dollars per hour and it would take him four to five hours to do the job. Keep in mind that the door cost a hundred dollars and he wanted me to pay him four hundred dollars to install it. Believe it or not, I actually considered it briefly (because the thought of doing it myself made me cringe), but I eventually turned him down and grudgingly went back to work on the door.

I spent about five painstaking hours on a freezing-cold porch, adjusting and readjusting the door until I finally had it installed and working properly. My kids came out and told me how cool it looked and proceeded to open and close it while commenting on my handiwork. In that moment I swelled with pride from overcoming the challenge, making sense of the problem, and persevering in solving it. It was a great feeling, one we all get when we succeed in solving complex tasks. As I looked back, I couldn't believe I'd almost given up after only an hour and almost been willing to pay an exorbitant amount of money to have someone else do it for me.

Making sense of problems and persevering in solving them (MP1) is a life skill that helps us become more successful in our personal and professional lives. We are constantly bombarded with problems and challenges that require an enormous amount of effort and cognitive demand on our part. It is only with our drive and determination that we muddle through until we find a solution. Perseverance is a trait that some people seem to possess innately, whereas others appear to have very little of it. We see this with our students as well. Some of them work with a fierce tenacity to figure things out, and others give up after writing their name on their paper. How do we help *all* students learn to make sense of problems and persevere in solving them?

Sense Making

Let's explore this practice standard by first looking at what it means to make sense of problems. This part of the standard goes well beyond expecting students to simply identify the correct operation in a word problem. In fact, the expectation is that students will develop and use a more mindful approach when working through a variety of mathematical tasks, challenges, and problems.

When working to develop and support MP1, we do not emphasize speed. When we do that, we can easily encourage bad habits and create the impression that faster is always better (Boaler, Williams, and Confer 2015). There is a time and place for working toward efficient strategies, but with MP1, students are encouraged to take a methodical approach as they uncover the meaning of a problem and look for entry points. They reflect on what they understand about the task while considering the known information and identifying what unknown information they must figure out to arrive at a solution.

This can be challenging for young students who have had little experience with formal problem solving and are still in the early stages of developing reading comprehension skills. Not that every problem or task students encounter is text based, but a large number of them have text elements such as written instructions, rules, or contexts. These are important considerations as we think about how we will help students in the primary grades learn to read problems or instructions for a task in ways that uncover all the information they need to have entry points in solving them.

The standard says that students need to "analyze givens, constraints, relation-ships, and goals." To do so, they must learn how to strategically read a problem and reflect on those components. Although this standard is about sense making and perseverance in problem solving, there is a small element that connects to the development of reading skills for primary-grade students.

In the case of word problems, consider what it takes for students to understand what is being asked of them. First, students need to decode the text accurately. This is not so much the case for kindergartners but with some curriculum materials, first and second graders may have to read and solve problems independently. Assuming children can decode the text, they must also have the ability to read for meaning so they understand the context of the problem.

Comprehending the context is what allows students to make concepts and op-erations more meaningful (Sullivan, Zevenbergen, and Mousley 2003). Once they understand the context, students need to learn how to filter the available informa-tion to sort the critical information from the extraneous material. By reflecting on the known information, students can discern what information is missing and then devise a plan for developing what the authors of the Common Core call a "solution pathway."

It's important to recognize that new and struggling readers have a hurdle to clear when it comes to making sense of text-based problems. For these students, it can be enormously beneficial to have support with reading the problem so they can have access to the mathematics. We don't want their challenges with reading to get in the way of their sense making in math class. Reading problems to students or having them work with partners who can read the text are two ways to address this need.

Next, we want to encourage students to restate a problem or act it out as a first step in understanding what it is asking them to do. We want to encourage them to consider the known and unknown information and to devise an entry point into the work. This might involve drawing pictures of the situation to understand the action of the operation, using manipulatives or other tools and representations to make sense of the mathematics and design solution pathways, or considering related problems they've previously encountered. This approach requires students to work from their own understanding and reflection and to strategically and me-thodically think about the problem from beginning to end.

Making sense of problems and persevering in solving them takes time. The goal is for students to become efficient and fluent problem solvers. But the key is to take the time in the primary grades to establish this mindful approach and cultivate it as students learn to become independent problem solvers.

If we want our students to develop good habits, how do we begin? What can teachers do to support students as they learn to make sense of problems? The following vignette from a kindergarten classroom is a good example of how to help support our young students in developing sound habits and making sense of problems. The approach the teacher takes is appropriate for first and second graders as well. Before you read the vignette, I encourage you to read the practice standard and then reflect on it as you consider how this teacher is helping her students work toward developing this standard for mathematical practice.

Focus Questions

1. In what ways does Ms. Allen support her students in making sense of the problem?

2. Some students know the answer right away, but Ms. Allen deemphasizes getting the correct answers during this exchange. How does this move help students develop a more thoughtful approach to problem solving?

3. What was the benefit of Ms. Allen not clarifying that it was a subtraction problem, but rather moving kids on to solve the problem?

Will 8 – 3 Give Me More?

Ms. Allen—Kindergarten, March

My kindergartners were working with a subtraction problem. Before this work, we had been doing a lot with addition but not so much formal work with subtraction. I was curious how my students would interpret and solve the problem. Subtraction is always harder for my students, so I wanted to present this problem with a context that was easy for them to understand. I had the story written on chart paper and called the students to the floor to introduce the problem.

EIGHT KIDS WERE PLAYING IN THE BLOCK AREA DURING CHOICE TIME. THREE KIDS GOT UP AND MOVED TO THE ART CENTER. HOW MANY STUDENTS WERE LEFT IN THE BLOCK AREA?

Teacher: Girls and boys, I have a problem of the day written on the chart paper for us to think about this morning. Before we begin, who can tell me how we go about working with a new problem?

I have been working with students for a while on the steps they should take when working on a problem. We had the steps listed on a chart on the wall, but I always begin our problems of the day by asking them to restate them. I find this really helps when working with kindergartners.

Jesse: We have to sit crisscross applesauce.

Teacher: Yes, that's very important to help us be better listeners. But once you're all being good listeners, what's the first step we should take to work with this problem?

Students, all calling out: Read it!

Teacher: Excellent, yes, we want to read it, but how should we read it?

Juan: Carefully.

Lauren: You need to make pictures in your head.

Teacher: Can you explain what you mean by that?

Lauren: You make a movie in your head.

Teacher: You mean we have to think about the problem like a movie or a story?

Lauren: (Nods.) So you can see it.

Teacher: Can someone else tell me how that helps us?

Zak: It tells you what's happening so you can do it.

Teacher: What do you mean by "so you can do it"?

Zak: Like if you have to plus or take away.

Teacher: If we picture the story in our heads and see what's going on, it will tell us whether we have to add or subtract? (The students nod in agreement.) Okay, I'm going to read the story and you can join in if you'd like. We'll read the problem, and then I want you all to close your eyes and get a picture of the story.

Many times for problems like this, I read a story to the class that represents either an addition or a subtraction situation. I don't want it to become a reading exercise, so I don't dwell too much on the reading elements apart from modeling careful reading and rereading of the problem. At this point in the year some kids can read along with me, but most tend to let me do it while they concentrate on understanding it.

Teacher: Who can tell me what they saw when I read that story?

Kaneka: I saw 8 kids building a castle with the blocks.

Teacher: Did you see anything else happen?

Kaneka: No.

Teacher: Who else?

Jonathan: I saw 8 kids playing with blocks and then Kelsie, Mikal, and Cade walked away to do art.

Teacher: You saw 3 kids leaving?

Jonathan: Yes, and I know the answer!

Teacher: That's good, but remember, we aren't looking for answers yet. It's exciting when we get answers right away, but it's a good habit to take our time and be good thinkers as well. Sometimes our fast answer might not be the right one. What do we know in this story?

Maddie: Eight kids are in the block area.

Sarah: And they are playing.

Juan: Three kids go to art.

Teacher: So we know there are 8 kids in the block area and 3 kids leave to go to art. What don't we know? What are we trying to figure out?

Ethan: How many stayed.

Teacher: Yeah. Do you think our answer is going to be greater than 8 or less than 8? Remember, greater means "more than" and less means "smaller than." Raise your hand for more than 8 . . . greater than 8. (About six kids raise their hands.) Raise your hand if you think the answer will be less than 8 . . . smaller than 8. (About nine kids raise their hands.) Raise your hands if you're unsure. (Three kids raise their hands.)

I wasn't really surprised by the range of ideas. We had been doing so much work with addition that kids were used to the answer always being greater than the first number in the problem. I decided to ask a few students to explain their reasoning to give me a sense of their thinking, but also to get students talking to each other about their ideas.

Teacher: Sarah, you had your hand up for greater than. Can you tell us why you think that?

Sarah: Eight plus 3 is 12.

Teacher: So you think we want to add these two numbers together?

Sarah: Yes.

Teacher: Who else thinks that this problem is one where we want to add the numbers together? (A few hands go up.) Maddie, you said the answer will be less than 8. Can you tell us why?

Maddie: Well, 8 kids play . . . 3 leave. So it's smaller.

Jonathan: It's take-away.

Teacher: How do you know?

Jonathan: 'Cause you're taking away the kids.

Teacher: Who else thinks this is a subtraction or take-away problem? (A large number of hands go up.) We seem to have some different ideas about what to do with this problem. I would like you to work with your math buddy to try to solve this problem. There are cubes at your tables if you'd like to use them to help you show what's happening in the problem. I'll come around and watch you as you work, and then we'll meet on the floor to talk about what we did.

Ms. Allen worked with the class all year to develop a set of steps they should take when solving problems. These steps were designed to help students slow down and really think about problems rather than jumping right into solving them. In making this a routine approach to solving problems, she provided students with a lot of practice and helped them develop a habit of mind for reading and solving problems.

We want our students to see problems as real-life events because contexts are one important way students make sense of them. When students can see the action of a problem, they are able to get a sense of what they need to do to solve it.

Ms. Allen encouraged this approach by asking kids to develop mental images of the story. She wanted them to see it as an actual event so the problem would make sense. She had students talk about what they saw so they could build a collective understanding of the situation.

Another important move Ms. Allen made was asking students to think about whether the answer was going to be greater or less than 8. This form of estimation helps students consider what a reasonable answer might be before they even attempt to solve the problem. If students think the answer should be less but end with a greater total, an internal alarm should go off letting them know something is wrong. This is another habit of mind that strong math students exhibit, and Ms. Allen is helping her students develop it very appropriately.

Additionally, by asking whether the answer is going to be greater or less than 8, Ms. Allen is having her students consider what operation might be at play and how the action of the problem can help them determine the correct operation to use. This work may take time with young students because you continually have to prompt them with questions, but consider the benefits of the approach. Ms. Allen's students are collectively making sense of the problem with her guidance before even attempting to solve it. She is demonstrating the kind of thinking we want all our students to exhibit independently when solving problems in hopes that it becomes second nature for them. As a result, her students will be more mindful when working on problems in the future.

Using some phrasing from the CCSMP, Ms. Allen was helping her students "make conjectures about the form and meaning of the solution and plan a solution pathway." They were thinking about what they knew and understood and reflected on what was being asked of them. In doing so, they began to develop accurate solution pathways that would help them arrive at the correct answer.

Of course, there were some students who immediately jumped at the answer. We certainly like to see that level of fluency with our students, and it's exciting to observe some kindergartners demonstrating efficient mental math strategies. However, Ms. Allen made a deliberate move here to put the answering of the problem on hold. Every teacher has students who can quickly calculate answers, but these students aren't necessarily the best mathematical thinkers. At times, these same students have difficulty once the numbers in a problem are larger or the structure of the problem becomes more complex. One reason some of them struggle later on is that they learned to put their brains on autopilot when the math was easier for them. They focused on getting answers rather than making meaningful math connections.

For example, imagine a second-grade student who is really good at two-digit addition. In a matter of seconds she can solve those problems using her mental math strategies. As her teacher, we would be extremely happy with her computation skills. As we work with story problems involving two-digit addition, this student flies through the work because she doesn't need to read the problems. She knows each problem calls for addition because that is what the class is working on, and she has fluent strategies to solve them.

However, this particular student is not getting the necessary practice of making sense of problems. In fact, she may be developing the bad habit of jumping to conclusions about the operation based on an assumption or a cursory reading of the problem. This works as long as the problems are predictable or simplistic. However, when presented with a more complex problem involving multiple operations, she may hit a wall because she has not developed patient problem-solving strategies.

When focusing on MP1, the goal is to help students develop the skills to make sense of problems. We might have to make accommodations for students who solve problems quickly so that they're doing independent work, which will help them develop good habits. We could give these students a blend of addition and subtraction problems so they can't assume there is only one operation at play. We could also give more complex problems that involve multiple operations. Either one of these strategies would require students to slow down and be more thoughtful and strategic in their approach to each problem.

Another effective move made by Ms. Allen was when she had her students discuss what they understood about the problem and what they thought they were supposed to figure out. Not every student had a clear understanding about the problem based on the reading and class discussion. Some thought it was an addition problem, and some seemed unsure. Yet she did not use this time to "teach" the students what the correct operation was. Instead, she had them get to work on it.

Rather than work to make sure all students knew what the operation was before they had a chance to work on the problem, she embraced the fact that there was disagreement and left it to the students to determine the operation on their own. As students worked on the problem with their partners, conversations about the action of the problem were happening at each table. Students were representing the problem using cubes and pictures and explaining their understanding to each other in an effort to convince their partners that it was a subtraction problem.

In the end, they all answered the problem correctly. However, the process of working to make sense of the problem with peers was extraordinarily powerful. If Ms. Allen had cleared up the students' confusion right away by simply telling them it was a subtraction problem, they probably would have answered the problem more quickly, but they would also have missed the rich experience of coming to that understanding on their own.

By downplaying the importance of finding the answer right away and emphasizing the importance of understanding the problem, Ms. Allen is helping all of her students develop good habits that they will carry with them as they progress through the grades.

Understanding the story context to make sense of problems is important, but it's not the only way in which students can grasp the essence of what a problem is asking. Another key component of sense making for primary-grade students involves the use of concrete objects such as manipulatives or other representations such as drawings, number lines, and hundreds charts. Young students have been using such tools for years. However, more recently they are being used more intentionally in classrooms as tools for sense making.

When I first started teaching second grade, I thought manipulatives such as interlocking cubes or hundreds charts were ways to help struggling students solve problems and to offer assistance for those who had not yet figured out how to solve problems numerically. I actually worked very hard to get kids away from using them as quickly as possible. I thought my job, as a second-grade teacher, was to move students away from concrete tools toward abstract reasoning, to prepare them for the demands of third grade. I have since learned about the importance of using concrete objects and representations as ways to help students make sense of new mathematical ideas and as a way of communicating and clarifying their understanding of problems and their solutions.

An important step in making full use of representations and manipulatives is understanding and appreciating how they can help students recognize what information a problem is communicating and what information is missing, and that different manipulatives and representations elicit different mathematical elements in a given situation. For example, consider the following second-grade scenario from a classroom I observed in October.

|| Focus Questions

1. Do their representations show the actions from the balloon task? If so, how? If not, what equation matches their representation?
2. What questions would provide more insight into students' understanding of the structure of the problem?

How Many Cubes Will Make It Crash?

Ms. Singh—Grade 2, October

Ms. Singh was using a three-acts math task as an alternative to traditional problem structures. The math-in-three-acts approach was developed by Dan Meyer, a former teacher who is now a math consultant and chief academic officer at Desmos, a start-up company in California that is designing the next generation of math education technology. With this approach, a math task is presented in three acts. The first act is the hook. It introduces the problem in a way that engages the learner but gives only minimal information in order to spark students' curiosity. Often the first act is introduced through pictures, a video, or a demonstration. The second act is where we seek the information needed to solve the problem and work toward a solution. And the third act is the "reveal," where we see the actual results. You can find out more about math in three acts here: blog.mrmeyer.com/2011/the-three-acts-of-a-mathematical-story/.

In this particular three-acts task, students saw a video of some helium balloons with a cup attached to them floating up to the ceiling. Next, they saw small cubes being placed in the cup, one at a time. After eighteen cubes were placed in the cup, the balloon was still touching the ceiling. The teacher then asked students what they noticed and wondered as a way to get them thinking about the scenario.

What's great about this approach is that there is no formal question or problem involved here in Act 1. Students are simply presented with a scenario and then asked what they notice and wonder (Hogan and Alejandre 2010). This process allows all students to have an entry point—they can notice a basic observation ("The balloon is red") or a more mathematical observation ("I noticed she put in eighteen cubes"). Act 1 also lays the groundwork for students to formulate their own questions. (How many cubes does it take to make the balloon drop? How many cubes will keep the balloon hovering in midair? How many cubes would it take to bring one balloon down?) Act 1 engages all learners on a level playing field and gets them discussing the available information in depth. In this particular class the following discussion took place:

Josie: I noticed a hot air balloon go up and then the lady is trying to get it down with cubes.

Audrey: Yeah, she put in 18 and it's still staying up.

Beckett: I thought it was 19.

Zev: No, it's 18. I counted. I know it's 18.

Teacher: Do you want to see it again to make sure? (She shows the video and the class counts together. It is definitely 18.)

Maya: I'm wondering how many cubes will make it crash.

Teacher: Great question.

Davis: I think it's like 36 or something.

Teacher: Why 36?

Davis: It's a trick. I bet they stopped the video halfway. Eighteen and 18 is 36.

Teacher: Davis thinks 36. What about the rest of you? What's your estimate? Turn and tell your neighbor.

After estimates were shared, the class watched the second video from Act 1 showing more cubes being added, but then it faded so we couldn't see exactly how many more were added, ending with one more cube being added and the balloon slowly descending. The teacher asked the class what they noticed and wondered now.

Sasha: I want to know how many more cubes she put in.

Oliver: How many cubes together? What's the whole amount?

Teacher: If you wanted to know what the whole amount was, what information would you need if we already know 18 cubes are in the cup?

Oliver: How many she put in next.

Teacher: And what if we wanted to figure out how many she added and we only knew there were 18 in the cup?

Owen: We could watch the last video. (He knows that in the third act we see the final amount.)

Teacher: (Laughs.) Yes, Owen. We can certainly watch the last video and see the answer. Good thinking. But what if we want to figure it out first before we see the last video?

Tessa: What was your question?

Teacher: If we know there are 18 in the cup and we want to find out how much more she added, what other information would we need to know?

Tessa: You mean like the total amount?

Teacher: If we knew the starting amount and the total amount, could we figure out how many were added?

Tessa: I think so. Yes. Like with take-away or something.

Teacher: This is great. We have two really good questions to explore. I guess the one we work on depends on what information we have. Let's see what we have.

At this point the teacher showed another clip for Act 2, which showed the cup landing on the ground. The person dumped the cubes on the ground and the video sped up, showing the cubes getting organized in two stacks of 10 with 7 left over.

Students: Ohhhh. It's 27.

Teacher: Yeah, it looks like 27 brought it down. Some of you were really close with your guesses. So what do we know?

Audrey: She put in 18, and 27 made it come down.

Teacher: What don't we know?

Maya: What she put in.

This task occurred in a second-grade classroom in October as students were being introduced to missing-addend problems. Ms. Singh had been working to introduce her students to various addition and subtraction situations from the CCSSM. This particular task is classified as an "add-to, change unknown" problem. With this structure we know the starting amount and the total amount and are trying to discover what the amount added is.

A key point in helping students make sense of the differences in problem structures is to help them see the part-whole relationships between the values in different addition and subtraction situations. In this particular problem, students know one part (the starting amount) and the whole (the total number of cubes). What they don't know is the other part (the number of cubes added to the cup). All students will be finding the difference between the whole (27) and one of the parts (18), and they will employ a variety of solution strategies to do so. However, to be successful, they need to understand the situation and understand the relationship between addition and subtraction so that they'll be confident about using subtraction or addition to solve the problem. One way students make sense of these relationships is through the use of manipulatives and representations.

Below are students' attempts to makes sense of and solve the balloon task. Looking at student work through the lens of how they are making sense of the task and understanding the relationships between the values can give you a big window into their knowledge and understanding of operations and how they interpret the values in the task. As you look at each example below, ask yourself the following questions:

1. What mathematics from the problem does their approach explicitly highlight?
2. Do their models or representations model the action of the problem? If so, how?
3. What questions would we ask students about their representation to gain more insight into their understanding of the structure of the problem?

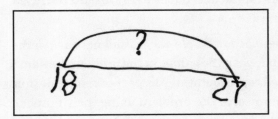

Figure 1.1 Paul

Paul: I started with 18 on one end and 27 on the other. I drew a line from 18 to 27 and put a question mark, because we don't know what number that is yet. But I didn't use the number line to solve it. I just did 18 plus 10 minus 1. (See Figure 1.1.)

Ryan: I started at 27 and took away 18. First I took away 7 to get to 20. Then I took away 10 to get to 10. Then I just had to take away 1 to get to 9. (See Figure 1.2.)

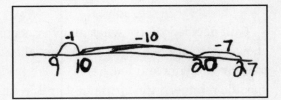

Figure 1.2 Ryan

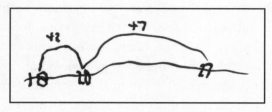

Figure 1.3 Gabby

Gabby: I started on 18 and then jumped up 2 to get to 20. Then I jumped up 7 to get to 27. Two plus 7 equals 9. (See Figure 1.3.)

Chelsea: I got 18 blue cubes and 27 yellow cubes. Then I matched up the cubes. If the cubes matched up, I could get rid of them. The cubes left over are the answer. (See Figure 1.4.)

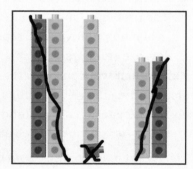

Figure 1.4 Chelsea

Figure 1.5 Lucas

Lucas: I started with 18 blue cubes and then added 2 yellow cubes to make 20. Then I kept adding more yellows until I got to 27. Then I just counted all the new cubes to get my answer. (See Figure 1.5.)

As you can see, there are multiple ways students can represent the relationship between the values in the problem. In some cases, students created representations as part of their solution pathway and went on to solve the problem using their number line or the cubes. Other students represented the problem to understand the operation and then chose numerical strategies to solve it.

Paul decided to use what many educators refer to as an "open number line" to show the relationship between the values. This unmarked number line is a great tool for students and teachers. Unlike traditional number lines that are fixed with specific numbers, the open number line can be constructed easily by drawing a line and inserting the relevant numbers for a given problem (Burns 2015).

In Paul's case, he used the open number line to represent distance. The two known quantities (18 and 27) are listed as points on the number line. The distance (or difference) between the two is represented as a jump between them. Paul's representation indicates that he understands the structure of the problem, because it shows he knows he can add up to find the difference. This idea is similar to Lucas's strategy in that he started with the 18 and added up to get to 27. I would like to ask Paul how he could show his mental math strategy on the open number line. My hunch is that he can, but we don't know unless we ask him.

Ryan also used the open number line, but represented the problem as removal. Although his approach does not match the action of the balloon task, it reveals the part-whole relationship among the quantities represented. MP1 doesn't specify that students directly model the actions in a task. The relationship between the values is much more important. When students understand that relationship, it offers many more options for them in terms of solution pathways and helps them develop flexible problem-solving strategies.

In this case, Ryan's representation shows an open number line with the 18 being removed in small chunks. According to his teacher, counting back is a preferred method for him, and decomposing the 18 into smaller chunks allowed him to find landmark numbers like 20 and 10. This is a good indication of his number sense and strategic thinking, because he realized he could decompose the 18 into manageable parts and purposefully broke it up so he would land on specific numbers. This representation also shows he understands the part/whole relationship of the values and that he can use subtraction to find the other part.

Gabby, like Paul and Ryan, used the number line, but in a different way. Unlike Paul, who solved the problem mentally and used the number line to show how he thought about the problem structure, and Ryan, who used it to show how he removed 18 in small parts, Gabby used the number line to add up to the whole amount. She started with the known part (18) and added on to it until she got to the known whole (27). She chose to move to a landmark number (20) the same way Ryan did. Her approach also captured the action of the balloon task where we start with 18 cubes, add some more, and have 27 cubes in the end.

Recall that Chelsea used a comparison approach between 18 and 27, shown in Figure 1.4. It's a little hard to see this because of the way she oriented the cubes on the Smartboard, but if we line them up differently, it is easier to see the comparison. (See Figure 1.6.)

Figure 1.6 Chelsea's cubes reorganized for comparison

She was looking to find the difference between 18 and 27 and was able to do it by matching up the blue and yellow cubes. She made 18 with a stack of 10 blue cubes and 8 more. She made 27 with two stacks of 10 yellow cubes and 7 more. Then she matched a blue stack of 10 with a yellow stack of 10 and removed them. Then she broke 1 off the stack of 8 blue cubes and matched the remaining 7 with the 7 yellow cubes. Then she removed those cubes. Finally, she took the 1 remaining blue cube and matched it with 1 yellow cube from the stack of 10 and removed those. She was left with 9 yellow cubes.

When written out, it sounds very complicated, but she completed those moves with relative ease. It's not the most efficient strategy, but it does indicate that she understands the relationship between the values. In this case, she saw the relationship as a comparison. Although this approach helped her arrive at her solution, I would want to ask her if there was a more efficient way she could compare the two quantities. I'm curious to see what she would do.

Finally, we see Lucas's model, where he started with the known part (18). He then added cubes, one at a time, until he got to the known total (27). His approach was similar to Gabby's in that he was understanding the problem as an "add-to, change unknown" structure. In this case, he was acting out the problem with the cubes. Although his approach to the task was not as efficient as Gabby's, his understanding of the problem and relationship between the values is strong, which is what we are looking for with MP1.

The above examples illustrate the range of representations students use to make sense of problems. At any given grade level, students have different needs and will make use of these tools in varying ways. Some, like Lucas and Chelsea, use the representation to make sense of the problem and do the computation. Others use more efficient representations that convey the relationship between the values but use other numerical strategies to do the computation, like Paul. In all cases, it was evident that the students understood the problem, and their representations helped suggest how they interpreted the relationship between the 18, 27, and 9. If we make representational tools available to all students, they will become more successful when learning how to interpret mathematical problems and tasks.

As students use various representations to make sense of problems, teachers should encourage them to share their ideas in math conversations. As different representations are shared, students should look for connections between them. You can ask questions such as "Are any two ways of thinking about this problem similar?" or more specifically, "How are Gabby's and Lucas's representations similar?" These kinds of questions help students connect to other representations and broaden their thinking. We should also connect representations to the story contexts to further students' understanding. Asking questions such as, "Can someone tell me a new story using Lucas's cube model?" will help students see how representations convey meaning.

This work takes time. It can be tempting to move through it quickly in an effort to get students to solve problems faster. However, when we accelerate the process, we leave many students behind. All students benefit from this work of using contexts and representations to make sense of problems and communicate understanding. In fact, more often than not, my second graders who were strongest with computation skills had difficulty connecting their work to any meaningful context or representation. They would simply solve a problem and say, "I just knew it." By having everyone engage in this work, we are able to help those students see the mathematics behind their quick problem-solving strategies. As we move into more complex work with larger numbers, they will carry this new understanding with them and have a deeper conceptual understanding of the mathematics as a result.

Perseverance

The second part of MP1 deals with students' abilities to stay with a problem to the end. As indicated in my story about the storm door, perseverance is a life skill that transcends mathematics; it's a mind-set worth fostering and developing. As primary-grade teachers, we are the first ones to present formal problem solving to students, and their experiences with us can help shape their attitudes for the future. It is critical that we support our students in developing both a mindful approach to problem solving and patience with the process. How do we do that?

One key strategy is to remember that less is more. When I went to school, math consisted of pages and pages of problems for us to solve. We would get a sheet with thirty of them on Monday and be told to solve all the even-numbered ones. Then on Tuesday we would solve the odd-numbered ones. The goal was speed and efficiency. We were praised if we finished quickly and were encouraged to take as many shortcuts as possible. I had a teacher who used to give us an index card so we could cover up all the numbers in the problem except for the column of numbers we were operating with at any given time (ones place, tens place, and so on). I can say for certain that this approach emphasizing speed did little to teach me perseverance. When I encountered a challenge, I got frustrated. And when I got frustrated, I gave up.

It's important for us to think about what we value as teachers and how we communicate that to our students. Rather than push the idea of speed, why not push the idea of thoughtfulness? Math should be minds-on all the time. That's not to say we should ignore the importance of efficiency—quite the contrary, in fact. We want all of our students to develop computational fluency, but to truly achieve that, we must encourage thoughtful approaches to mathematics. Instead of praising students for how fast they solve problems, we should talk about how well students solve problems. Our students look to us for guidance. They pick up on what we value and what we deem important. If we value sense making and perseverance, they will work to develop those traits.

When students exhibit a mindful approach to solving a task or demonstrate some mental fortitude after encountering a setback, we want to point it out to them so they see that we value their approach (Boaler 2013). We might say things such as "I noticed you solved the problem two different ways. How did that help you know you had the right answer?" or "I saw you were working really hard to make sure you found all the solutions to the problem." By making statements and asking questions that highlight these behaviors, students learn that they are important and will be more likely to work to develop them.

Consider the following vignette from a first-grade classroom as an example of supporting students in persevering through this challenging problem:

> **I HAVE 12 MARBLES IN THIS SHOE BOX. SOME OF THE MARBLES ARE RED AND SOME OF THE MARBLES ARE BLUE. HOW MANY OF EACH COLOR COULD BE IN THIS BOX?**

Problems like this are ideal for supporting students in developing the behaviors listed in MP1—there are multiple solutions and various ways students can approach this task. This problem also allows for diverse entry points, depending on the knowledge and skills of the individual students. As you read the vignette, pay attention to what the teacher says to the children as they are working.

Focus Questions

1. How does the teacher support her students in developing perseverance when problem solving?
2. How does she use the experience of two students to support perseverance with her whole class?

Ugh, That'll Take Forever

Ms. Turner—Grade 1, November

I began this lesson by showing students a shoe box I brought in that had 12 marbles in it. I explained that some of the marbles were blue and some of the marbles were red. I then asked how many of each color could be in the box. This problem was new to students, because until this point, we had worked only with problems that had one solution. For this problem, there were eleven possible combinations of marbles. I was curious to see how my students would approach the problem. Would they see that there was more than one answer? Would they attempt to find other solutions or stop at one? Would they approach this problem strategically or just make random attempts at combinations? I did not want to lead them too much, so my introduction to the problems involved just my initial presentation with the shoe box and asking kids to comment on what they had to figure out. I then set them to work with their math partners and walked around to observe their work.

The first pair I visited was June and Amelia. They had 12 red cubes and 12 blue cubes on their table. June began by putting 10 red cubes in the center of the table, and Amelia matched them with her blue cubes. They then wrote *10 blue marbles* and *10 red marbles* on their paper. I decided to join the conversation.

Teacher: Can you tell me what you did?
June: I got 10 of my cubes, and she put 10 of her cubes in. Then we wrote it down.
Teacher: Why did you choose 10?
June: It's a friendly number.

I think they were used to me asking them about tens a lot, so perhaps they just assumed they needed to work with tens here. First graders can sometimes overgeneralize concepts in an effort to do what they think I want them to do.

Teacher: Let's think about the problem we are working on. What can you tell me about it?

Amelia: You have red and blue marbles in that box.

Teacher: You are right, and I noticed you actually got red and blue cubes to show that. What else do we know?

June: There are 12 marbles.

Teacher: What don't we know?

Amelia: (Short pause.) How many blues and reds.

Teacher: Exactly. We don't know how many reds I have or how many blues I have. But what do we know?

June: You have marbles.

Teacher: How many?

June: Twelve.

Teacher: Okay, so I have 12 marbles altogether. Let's look at your first solution.

Amelia: Oops. Too much. (She counts out 12 blue cubes.)

June erases their paper and writes 12. They then look at me as if to say, "Now what?"

Teacher: Are you finished?

June: I think so.

Amelia: No, wait. We didn't do red.

Teacher: Is that important?

Amelia: Didn't you say you had red ones too?

Teacher: Yes.

Amelia (to June): We need red.

June appears to be getting frustrated. She likes to fly through work—and not just in math. I have to stay on her so she will push herself, but she gets frustrated easily. I can see it starting here. She begins erasing her paper.

Teacher: Do you have an idea of what could be in the box, June?

June: I don't know. Like 10 blues and (counts up on her fingers) 2 reds.

Amelia: Oh yeah. Good one.

Teacher: So that works? (Amelia nods while June writes it down.)

June: Are we done?

Amelia: Well, there could be other answers. (June groans.)

Teacher: What's wrong, June?

June: This is going to be hard.

Teacher: Why?

June: Because there can be like a hundred answers.

Amelia: Yeah. Numbers go on forever.

Teacher: This can seem like a big problem. Does that mean you have to come up with a hundred answers?

June: Maybe.

Teacher: Well, let's stop to think about this problem. How many marbles did you say she had?

Amelia: Twelve.

Teacher: Would it make sense that she could have over a hundred different combinations of red and blue marbles if she has 12 marbles?

June: Not really. But there's still a lot.

Teacher: How could you approach this problem so it doesn't seem overwhelming?

Amelia: We can take turns. She can put some of her cubes down and then I can, and then we switch.

June: Do I have to do all the writing?

Amelia: We can take turns.

June: Okay.

Teacher: I notice you are coming up with a plan to solve this problem. I'm going to visit some other groups and then come back to you to see how you're doing.

I wanted to give them time to sit with it. The problem seems daunting at first, but they were on their way to developing a good approach. I know June gets easily overwhelmed with extra work and tends to rush through things. That's why I paired her with Amelia, who tends to be more thorough and usually solves problems in more than one way. I thought she might be a good role model for June. I visited other groups and saw a range of approaches. Some groups were just as flustered as June and Amelia, whereas others approached the problem strategically and seemed to have a way to determine every possible combination.

When I returned to June and Amelia, they had much more on their paper. I watched them work together. First June would pick a random number of red cubes. In this case it was 3. Then Amelia counted on from there as she added blue cubes. She counted out 9 blue cubes and then wrote *3 red and 9 blue*. Their paper had the following information on it (see Figure 1.7):

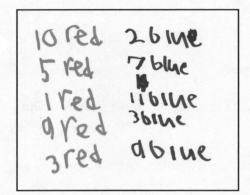

10 red   2 blue
5 red   7 blue
1 red   11 blue
9 red   3 blue
3 red   a blue

Figure 1.7   June and Amelia's work

They had made a lot of progress, but I noticed they were using a more random approach. It appeared that June would just pick a random number of red cubes and Amelia would build from there. I decided to check in with them to see how they were feeling about the problem.

Teacher: How's it going?
June: Good. I think we have enough.
Teacher: Did you find all the combinations?
June: All? (Groans.) That'll take forever.
Teacher: Well, it looks like you've made a lot of progress already. Do you think you found them all?
Amelia: Not all, but we're close.
Teacher: How can you tell?
June: We already did a lot.
Teacher: I see that. Are there any you haven't used yet?
June: Six and 4 (She proceeds to write 6 red and 4 blue on her paper.)
Amelia: That's not right. Six and 4 make 10. It should be 6 and 6.
June: Oh yeah. (She fixes the error.)
Teacher: I see that you two are doing some really hard thinking. You are remembering the 12 as your total and paying attention to which numbers you are using. How is that helping you?
Amelia: If we use each number, then we know we found them all.
Teacher: So your plan is to try each number? Does it seem as overwhelming now that you have a plan, June?
June: Not really. I think we're close. (She is smiling at this point and starting to look for another example.)
Teacher: That seems like a good plan. Can I have you share your plan with the rest of the class when we talk about our work at the end of class? I'm really proud of you two, because it can be frustrating when it looks like we have a big job to do. But neither of you gave up. You came up with a good plan and made the job easier. Can you talk about that too when you share?
Both: Sure!

I was happy to see that they did not give up. June seemed ready to throw in the towel because she appeared to have enough examples. However, once she had a chance to think through a plan to know whether they had them all, she got a burst of energy. I think she needed to see that the problem had an end point and didn't just go on forever. The two of them tried every combination with cubes until they found them all.

In the end, we came together as a class and the two of them shared their strategy of making sure they tried every number (1–11) for each color. Although their approach jumped around based on the particular number June picked, they did account for each number they tried. I then had another group share their strategy. Alexis and Paige started with 11 red cubes and 1 blue cube and then worked down from there (10 red and 2 blue, 9 red and 3 blue, and so on). I then asked the class to compare how Alexis and Paige's strategy was similar to and different from June and Amelia's.

June: It's like the same but theirs was way easier.
Teacher: How so?
June: 'Cause they just went down from here (pointing to the initial 11 red). That's wicked easy. I wish we had done that.

June was very excited to see this more streamlined approach, and I am sure she will use it for future problems like this. I think she just needed to approach the problem a bit more strategically by thinking about what the goal was. At first it seemed the problem was endless and daunting, but as she talked through it, the structure began to make sense. Then it no longer seemed impossible and she had a clear goal to work toward. Sometimes that's all we need.

The teacher in this vignette, Ms. Turner, did an amazing job of supporting the students as they tackled a complex problem and struggled to stay with it. What is noticeable is that she and her students spent an entire class period on just one problem. She set the expectation that they would all work to find multiple solutions to the one problem. That alone creates a class culture that encourages thoughtfulness and patience. Additionally, she set them to work without showing them a procedure for determining all the possible combinations. Leaving a bit of ambiguity in a problem is helpful when trying to encourage students to make sense of the task and persevere in tackling it. She gave them enough support to give them a way into the problem, but left a lot to be discovered by the students.

Once they were working, she visited with other small groups and engaged them in similar conversations. Most of the interactions involved the teacher asking students probing and clarifying questions to push them along in their thinking. The teacher then helped the students articulate their thinking. Her questions helped the students consider what they knew about the problem and what they had to find out. She never pointed out that their first solution was incorrect. Instead, she asked them to describe what they did and then compare it with what they knew about the problem. In doing so, she was helping them internalize some of the behaviors I listed above. The students saw their error and corrected their strategy.

Once they had a new approach, the teacher moved on to observe other students. Upon returning to June and Amelia, she noticed they had made more progress but also recognized that June was getting frustrated. She acknowledged June's feelings and helped redirect her thinking to be more strategic. Again, she used great questions to move their thinking along. Additionally, she validated their efforts by asking them to share their approach with the rest of the class.

During the wrap-up discussion, the teacher helped different groups connect their thinking by asking students to consider the similarities and differences in both approaches. June and Amelia had an effective strategy that accounted for all combinations, but the lack of order meant they had to do a lot of rechecking to see if they had used all the numbers. Alexis and Paige had a more methodical strategy that also involved using all numbers 0–12. However, they went a step further to do the problems in succession. By connecting the two approaches, June (as well as all the students) could see the value in using a strategic approach.

This emphasis on perseverance was the norm for Ms. Turner's classroom. That was how they approached problem solving all year. Students would work just a few problems at a time and then discuss their strategies as a group. By making this the norm, the teacher spent the year encouraging students to be mindful and patient problem solvers.

MP1 sets the stage for how students approach problem solving. It encourages a methodical and thoughtful approach. Math is supposed to make sense for students, and this standard communicates that math is not solely about answer getting. Mathematically proficient students don't blindly apply formulas and algorithms in an effort to find a quick solution. Instead, they purposefully analyze problems, consider known and unknown information, and devise a plan for arriving at a solution. They may apply efficient methods to solve the problem, but it's done with intention and mindfulness.

Mathematically proficient students also show resolve when encountering challenges or setbacks. They revise their thinking and check their work with multiple methods. If their current solution pathway leads to a dead end, they readjust their approach and start again without giving up. Throughout the process they continually ask themselves if the math makes sense. If it does, they continue with their work. If it doesn't, they seek to find meaning in their work through the use of representations or manipulatives.

Primary students do not come to school packaged with this mind-set. For them, problem solving is a new venture and they are just beginning to develop the skills and mind-sets for this work. We support them in this endeavor by valuing a strategic and mindful approach to solving mathematical problems. We demonstrate this approach constantly as we engage in math tasks together, and we reinforce this thinking as we see students applying MP1 in their own work.

As you begin to emphasize MP1 in your classroom, you may find it helpful to use anchor charts that you create with your students. You can begin by asking them how they make sense of problems. What helps them? Then you can list their ideas and add your own to create a chart called "How We Make Sense of Problems." As students begin work on tasks, you can have them refer to the chart as a way to prime their thinking. Anchor charts like these clearly communicate to students that we value this approach and that making sense of the math is important.

You can do the same thing to support students in persevering when problem solving. I had a chart in my classroom titled "What to Do When You're Feeling Stuck." Each year the chart had different ideas because they were created with the students, but generally we had ideas such as these:

- Read the question or directions again.
- Draw a picture of what we know.
- Ask a friend for help.
- Use math tools.
- Ask a teacher for help.
- Try smaller numbers first.

As with the anchor chart for making sense of problems, the perseverance chart provides another layer of support for students and communicates that they have lots of options to help them when they are stuck. It also lets them know that getting stuck, making mistakes, not knowing how to start, and so on are all part of the problem-solving process. All of us get stuck. Part of problem solving is using our resources and trying other strategies to help us get unstuck.

Whether we're solving a math task or installing a storm door, slowing down and making sense of the problem, creating a strategic plan, and working through challenges and setbacks means we can persevere and be successful. This habit of mind takes time to develop, but when we engage in the work and experience success, our mindful approach is reinforced by the great feeling we get when we persevere. As primary-grade teachers, we set the stage for these experiences and lay the groundwork for students to make sense of problems and persevere in solving them—in math and in life.

CHAPTER 2

Mathematical Practice 2: Reason Abstractly and Quantitatively

A few years ago I was having dinner with a group of friends at a restaurant in Washington, D.C. It was a trendy place that served eccentric small-plate entrees such as roasted quail on waffles and pork belly beignets (yes, you read that right). Although the menu made for some interesting dining, our dinner conversation actually focused on the floor of the restaurant. The entire floor was made of pennies held in place with some kind of sealant. When our waiter came over, he said they were having a contest asking people to guess the total number of pennies used to design the floor, with the person with the closest answer being the winner. My friends and I, all fiercely competitive, jumped on this opportunity to win a free dinner.

While we worked, I noticed that people at other tables were doing the same thing. I saw them pointing and counting, motioning to particular areas of the floor, and generally having a great time with the challenge. As I eavesdropped on the neighboring conversations, the range of strategies and estimates struck me. Some people were very methodical as they determined the total amount for a small area and then reasoned how much would cover a larger area. Others focused on anomalies within the restaurant's architecture that would affect the general area. Some simply threw out an estimate based on gut instinct rather than making any specific calculation. Regardless of the approach, the patrons in the restaurant had a wide range of skills and strategies to tackle the contest, and many were reasoning abstractly and quantitatively.

Mathematical Practice 2, Reason Abstractly and Quantitatively, focuses on students' abilities to make sense of quantities and their relationships in problem situations. In other words, students need to understand what each number in a problem represents and how the numbers relate to one another and to the operation(s) at work in the problem. As I said in Chapter 1, solving problems is not about blindly performing calculations without thinking. Learning rote procedures without understanding does not help our students become efficient and effective problem solvers. We want them to understand quantitative relationships so they can develop flexible and useful strategies to solve problems.

At the restaurant in D.C., there were a lot of values to consider: the length and width of the dining room, the general area of a penny, the number of pennies that could cover a square foot, and so on. To tackle the penny problem, we needed to determine the relationship between the values. In this case, we estimated that 16 pennies covered a 12-inch line. Therefore, a 12-by-12-inch space would have 16 rows of 16 pennies; 16 x 16 = 256. From there we estimated the length and width of the dining room to calculate the square footage and then multiplied that by 256. We understood the quantities involved in the problem and their relationship to one another. We also kept track of which numbers referred to which units and considered how the different units related to one another. All of this information helped us reason through the penny problem.

An example of MP2 can be seen when Mr. Rath presented his first graders with a challenge to determine the total number of hands of the students in the class. One student, Edith, understood that she had to add a series of twos together because each student in her class had two hands. She also understood that the number of students in the room determined the number of twos added together. She chose to represent this situation by writing 2 + 2 + 2 + 2 + 2 + 2 + 2 + 2 + 2 + 2 + 2 + 2 + 2 + 2 + 2 + 2 + 2 + 2 + 2 + 2 = 40. In this case, she took a real context (hands in her classroom) and represented it quantitatively. Her partner, Michael, approached the same task by reasoning that five kids sat at every table group, so each group had ten hands. There were four groups altogether, so he represented the problem as 10 + 10 + 10 +10 = 40. In both cases, the students considered the different values in the task and how they related to one another. They also had to keep track of which numbers referred to hands/people or hands/groups.

The way in which Edith and Michael approached the task illustrates the first key feature of this standard for mathematical practice: "to abstract a given situation and represent it symbolically and manipulate the representing symbols as if they have a life of their own, without necessarily attending to their referents." In other words, students need opportunities to *decontextualize* problems by representing situations with numbers and symbols.

Instead of counting the hands in the classroom, the students represented them abstractly in groups of 2 or groups of 10. When they represented the hand problem with a mathematical expression, they may not have attended to the fact that each number represented a group of hands while they were performing their calculations. But once they performed the calculation, they needed to return to the problem context to answer the question, "How many hands are in our class today?" Furthermore, both Edith and Michael were able to go back to their expressions and say what each symbol referred to in terms of the context. They hadn't completed the thinking once they finished the calculation.

This idea of decontextualizing tasks is challenging for students in the primary grades who are just beginning to make sense of numbers, quantities, and operations. We know they eventually need to learn to operate numerically if they are going to develop computational fluency, but a lot of groundwork needs to be laid before that can happen. That's why much of our work as primary-grade teachers must also emphasize the second key component of MP2: the ability to *contextualize* an abstract task or problem. Young students make sense of mathematics through visual representations and story contexts. We want to encourage our students to visualize and/or contextualize problems in an effort to understand what the numbers and symbols represent.

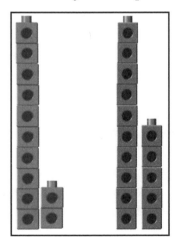

Figure 2.1 Cube representation

To make sense of an abstract problem, students apply a contextual surround to give the quantities meaning. For example, to understand 12 + 15 = ___, a student might imagine having 12 pencils in her desk and a friend giving her 15 more. The story context serves as a meaningful backdrop from which she can think about the two known quantities and the action of addition. Using this story, she might reason that the resulting answer will be greater than 12 because she started with 12 pencils and gained 15 more. She might also visually represent the problem using cubes or actual pencils so she can see what the two quantities represent before physically combining them to model the action of addition. (See Figures 2.1 and 2.2.)

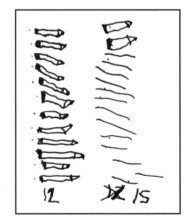

Figure 2.2 Pictorial representation

In this way, MP2 relates to MP1 in terms of students understanding a problem. In the previous chapter, we discussed how students make sense of problems by using representations and contexts. However, MP2 goes beyond students understanding the problem by focusing on *how* students view the quantities in the problem (their relationship to each other and their relationship to the problem structure and operations involved). The students' use of story contexts in this case can help them think about the quantities differently from the way they are presented in the original problem of 12 + 15.

For example, they might envision that pencils come in boxes of 10. Therefore, in their story, they start with one box of 10 pencils with an additional 2 single pencils (see Figure 2.3). Their friend gives them another box of 10 pencils with an additional 5 single pencils. This contextualization of the problem helps the student think about the quantities differently and supports them in developing a strategy that relies on numerical reasoning to solve the problem.

1 box of 10 pencils + 1 box of 10 pencils = 20 pencils

2 individual pencils + 5 individual pencils = 7 individual pencils

20 pencils + 7 pencils = 27 pencils

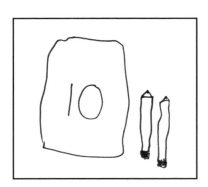

Figure 2.3 Pictorial representation using boxes of 10

By envisioning the pencils coming in boxes of ten, students can add the quantities together using a place-value method in which they add the tens first and then the ones, and combine the results to get the total sum. The story supports the reasoning because it provides a purpose for the pencils to be broken up into tens and ones.

Contexts such as pencils that come in boxes of ten or scenarios involving dimes and pennies help students make sense of addition strategies based on place value because they are rooted in the students' experiences. As primary students develop their understanding of the base ten number system, they should have plenty of opportunities to contextualize the base ten structure to give it meaning. Any familiar context in which objects are grouped in tens and ones will help students make sense of this numerical structure. Once they understand that structure, they can begin to develop problem-solving strategies based on place value.

MP2 specifies that mathematically proficient students should be able to move between contextualizing and decontextualizing situations as it suits their needs. These two processes are not exclusive of each other, and students often jump between the two as illustrated in the hand problem above. Although students were presented a contextualized situation involving hands, they decontextualized the situation by considering groups of two or groups of ten. After performing the calculation numerically, they contextualized their result by referring to forty as the total number of hands in the classroom.

The essence of this mathematical practice lies in students' abilities to *reason*—to make use of all they know and understand about numbers and operations. This seems like a tall order when we consider that our students are fairly new to the mathematical world and the depth and breadth of their knowledge is just emerging. However, even our youngest students can and should use what they know in both familiar and novel situations. They just need to be given opportunities to do so.

K–2 teachers are charged with laying the foundation for students' mathematical reasoning. This work takes time, it's messy, it's rooted in concrete materials and familiar contexts, and it's incredibly important for our students' future success. As with all the practice standards, there are no specific, prescribed ways to implement and support them in the classroom, but it is often helpful to have some examples of what you can do with your students. What follows are examples of ways to support K–2 students as they learn to reason abstractly and quantitatively. The classroom vignettes will give you particular views of this work, but you are encouraged to think about how these ideas will play out in your classroom as well.

Supporting the Foundational Knowledge

If students are going to learn to reason abstractly and quantitatively, they must have a strong foundation in number, operations, and base ten. These are the building blocks of computational fluency, and one of our biggest charges as primary teachers is to ensure that our students gain a strong understanding in these key ideas. That means we cannot rush through concepts in an effort to get students using numerical strategies faster. Imagine if construction workers decided to blow through the process of laying a foundation for a skyscraper they were building. We know they would end up with a building that was not structurally sound. The same is true for mathematics. We don't want our students to move on from the primary grades with a fragile understanding of these critical areas.

The very first part of MP2 says that mathematically proficient students "make sense of quantities." That means that students understand what numbers mean and represent. They know that the number 7 represents 7 objects. They know that 7 balls is the same number of objects as 7 blocks. They know that 7 can be decomposed into lots of smaller combinations of numbers (6 + 1, 5 + 2, 4 + 3, 3 + 4, 2 + 5, 1 + 6, 3 + 2 + 2, and so on). They know 7 comes right after 6 and right before 8 on a number line. They know that the number 7 is three away from a landmark number (10).

Young students come to understand quantities by having lots of experiences with counting. As they work to count concrete objects, they begin to solidify their understanding that numbers represent a specific value. Students cannot reason abstractly and quantitatively if they have weak number sense, so a big part of working toward this practice standard is helping them deepen their understanding of quantities. Therefore, activities where students have to count things are helpful in laying the foundation for MP2 because they are connecting abstract numbers to concrete objects or pictures.

The following vignette shows an example of a teacher supporting this early work with her kindergartners. As you read, reflect on the focus questions and consider your own experiences in your classroom.

Focus Questions

1. How are Ms. Hildago's students making sense of quantities?
2. What are the benefits of not letting students do direct comparisons of the objects in the counting bags?
3. As you look at Ms. Hildago's observations of her students, what does each child seem to understand and what ideas do they still need to develop?

Are There More T. Rexes Than Puppies?

Ms. Hildago—Kindergarten, May

My little kindergartners love our counting station. It's a place in our math corner where we have lots of counting activities set up, such as inventory lists on which students keep track of our community supplies such as pencils and erasers; counting bags full of fun things to count; mystery counting boxes, into which students stick their hands so they can count the mystery objects and guess what they are; and our *Count and Compare Challenge*, where students count the objects in two counting bags and compare the two quantities to see which bag has more objects.

For the previous two days, students had been working on a variety of counting challenges, but I was particularly interested in how they were doing with the *Count and Compare Challenge*. I had one bag with 9 plastic toy puppies and 11 plastic carnivorous dinosaurs. For this activity, students needed to count the objects in both counting bags and write the totals on their *Count and Compare* sheet. They then had to determine which bag had more objects and how many more. This is not easy for many of these youngsters, who are still developing counting strategies.

Comparing quantities is complicated work, and I made it more challenging by not allowing them to directly compare the actual objects in the bags. They had to dump out the objects in one bag, count them any way they wanted, and write the total number on their recording sheet (see Figure 2.4). After that they had to put the objects back into the bag. Then they repeated the process for the second set of objects. This way, students could not just dump out both bags and line the objects up. I wanted them to have to decontextualize the objects into two quantities and, if needed, contextualize them again using other materials.

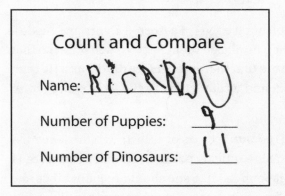

Figure 2.4 Recording sheet

Once they were finished with the first part of the task, they had to work on the actual comparison at their seats. All they had on their sheets at this point were the two totals they had come up with during the counting part of the task. If they needed physical objects to compare, they had to re-create the total amounts with manipulatives such as cubes and compare them. My thinking was that if I didn't let students do a direct comparison at the counting station, it might help them think about how to re-create a context for 9 and 11 or for me to require them to do another form of comparison.

As students worked on all the math activities for this last day, I walked around with my clipboard, observed them working, and took notes. I did not intervene because I wanted to see the range of responses for this problem. My plan was to have the class discussion at the end focus on this particular problem; we would clear up any misconceptions then. Below are a few of the observations I made during the working time.

Sophia: Sophia returned to her seat with correct totals on her sheet. She then took out a box of cubes and counted out 9 blue cubes to represent the puppies and 11 red cubes to represent the dinosaurs. She moved the blue cubes to one side of her table and the red cubes to the other side. She then wrote *Dogs are more* on her sheet. I asked her why she thought there were more puppies. She said that they were bigger. (I think she meant they took up more space.) When I looked at her table, the blue cubes were spread out more and the red cubes were condensed into a tight pile. To answer the question of how many more, she just wrote *9* because there were 9 blue cubes.

Ricardo: Ricardo took his paper to the class number line taped to the board in the front of the room. He quickly wrote that there were more dinosaurs. I asked how he knew and he said, "Because 11 is more than 9." He then put his finger on the 9 on the number line and counted the 9, 10, and 11. He then wrote that there were 3 more dinosaurs on his paper.

Dante: Dante worked with cubes. He took out 9 cubes of assorted colors and made a stack of them. He did the same for 11. Then he placed them next to each other so that the bottoms of the stacks lined up. He wrote that there were more dinosaurs. He then counted the 2 extra cubes in the 11 stack and wrote *2* next to the *How many more?* question.

Zoe: Zoe grabbed 9 counting bears and 10 counting bears of assorted colors (she miscounted the dinosaurs). Her tablemate, Chloe, quickly pointed out that there were 11 dinosaurs. She looked at me, and I said it sounded like she should recount since she had come up with one number and her friend suggested another number. She went back to recount and returned saying that she was wrong, and took out an extra bear. She then put them all back and began taking out just the blues while counting out loud, "One, two, three . . ." She continued taking more blue bears from the box until she counted to 9. She did the same thing with the green bears except she made sure she had 11. She wrote that there were more dinosaurs. Then she started to pair 1 blue bear with 1 green bear until she was out of blue bears. She counted the remaining green bears and wrote *2* next to the *How many more?* question.

Eliza: Eliza returned to her seat and wrote that there were more dinosaurs. When I asked how she knew, she said that 11 comes after 9, so it's bigger. When I asked her how many more dinosaurs, she quickly replied with 2. I asked how she knew and she said, "Because it's 10, 11. It's 2 away." She held up two fingers when she counted aloud.

There was quite a range of responses. Most students in the class did some kind of direct modeling, but some used alternative methods such as the number line or their own mental math strategies. I called the class to the rug for a brief discussion about the activity. My goal was to have some of the alternative ways to compare numbers beyond direct comparison come up during the discussion. That's not to say I don't want students doing direct comparison—I think it helps students solidify their number sense and practice contextualizing abstract situations—but I want them to connect with other representations of numbers and values.

Teacher: First of all, let's answer the big question. What did you discover when you worked on the *Count and Compare Challenge* today?

Sophia: The puppies were more. (One other student nods in agreement.)

Kiara: No they weren't. T. rexes are more than puppies.

Teacher: We have some disagreement here. Are there more T. rexes than puppies? (Most say yes.) Let's look at our work and see if we can all come to agreement.

I began the sharing portion of this discussion by having a few students share their work from creating equivalent sets. This approach was similar to the direct comparison approach because they lined up objects to compare them with one another versus working with abstract numbers. During this time Sophia agreed with her classmates that there were more dinosaurs, but she wasn't too sure. I didn't want to use this moment to work further with her, but I made a note to work with her more on it in the coming days. After students were finished sharing, I moved to the alternative approaches.

Teacher: Most students used counters to compare 9 and 11 to see how many more dinosaurs there were. But some of you tried new ways to solve this problem. Let's see a few of these strategies. Ricardo?

Ricardo: I used the number line. There's 9 here (points) and 11 here (points).

Teacher: How did you get 3 as your answer?

Ricardo: Just 1, 2, 3. (Counts up the 9, 10, and 11.) I don't know why I get 3.

Teacher: Good question. Some of you got 2, but Ricardo got 3 with the number line. Can someone else who tried the number line offer an idea?

Kevin: He did an extra. It goes there and there. See? Two.

Teacher: (I wasn't sure what he was referring to.) Can you come up and show us what you mean?

Kevin: (Walks up to the number line.) He went (points to the 9) 1, 2, 3 to 11. But it's 1, 2 (pointing to the 10 and 11). He did extra.

Ricardo: Ohhhh.

I'm not convinced Ricardo totally understood where he had gone wrong. He knew he had made a mistake, and Kevin's explanation seemed to get him thinking, but he's going to need more experience working with the number line before he really gets it. I made a note about it and continued the conversation.

Teacher: How does the number line help us see how many more 11 is compared with 9? (There was a long moment of silence at this point. I was thinking I needed to rephrase my question when Rachel spoke up.)

Rachel: You can just see it. See? They're next to each other, but 11 is higher. Then you go up 2 to that number.

Teacher: That's interesting. You're saying that the number line helps us compare the two numbers because we can see how far they are when they're next to each other? (Rachel and others nod.) Now, someone else had another way to think about this problem. Eliza, can you share what you did?

Eliza: I used my fingers.

Teacher: Yes, but can you explain how you thought about the problem?

Eliza: Eleven is bigger so I went 10 (holds up one finger), 11 (holds up another finger). See? (Holds up two fingers.) One, 2.

Teacher: You just counted from the smaller number until you got to the bigger number?

Eliza: Mm-hmm.

Teacher: Can someone else tell us what Eliza did? Caleb?

Caleb: She went 10, 11. (He models what she did with her fingers.)

Teacher: How are Eliza and Ricardo's strategies similar? What's the same?

Zoe: They both counted.

Teacher: Ricardo counted 2 on the number line starting at the 9, and Eliza counted 2 on her fingers starting at 9?

I realized at the end I had put words in Zoe's mouth, which is not really helpful, but I was running short on time and my students were becoming wiggly, which is my signal to wrap it up.

Teacher: I am very impressed with your work today. You were all able to count the objects in the counting bags and then compare the totals to see which was more and how many more it had. Some of you used counters to compare the two numbers, and a few tried new strategies just looking at the numbers on the number line or hundreds chart. We'll keep doing this work for the next few days so we get even better at it. Give yourselves a nice pat on the back for your hard work today.

My plan moving forward is to give them more opportunities to compare numbers. Some tasks will be similar to the *Count and Compare Challenge*, where they have to count physical objects, but I will encourage students to work with numbers to make the comparison so they begin to connect the quantities to the numbers that represent those quantities. My students need practice decontextualizing situations.

I will also give them raw number comparison situations that they will have to represent with cubes or a story so they can also practice contextualizing number situations. My goal is to get my students to see that they can move between working with objects or stories and working with numbers as it suits their needs.

These young students are developing the foundational understanding that will allow them to reason abstractly and quantitatively. Ms. Hildago understands that her students need rich experiences in counting and working with quantities, and she supports them by giving them activities that require them to bridge the space between physical quantities and abstract numbers. They have to count lots of objects and pictures and then represent the totals in numerical form. She also gives them numbers and has them create that amount with manipulatives and pictures.

In this particular vignette we see that Ms. Hildago even has students look at other representations of quantity such as the number line. This helps them see the number 9 as 9 objects and as a position on the number line. With this work evolving over the school year, you know her students will leave kindergarten with the strong foundational understanding of quantity that is necessary if they are to use numerical reasoning to solve problems when they are older.

Ms. Hildago supports MP2 by requiring her students to decontextualize the work with counting bags. Rather than let them count both groups and do a direct comparison at the same time, she asked that students count the items in each bag separately and write the numbers that represented the totals for both bags. As a result, all students returned to their seats with the numbers 9 and 11 on their paper rather than a physical representation of 9 and 11. She left the problem open in terms of how students would solve it, which allowed most of them to contextualize the problem again by representing it with physical quantities. It may seem like an extra step, but this is critical in helping students move between the physical and abstract.

Young students need lots of opportunities to do this to develop their number sense.

Also, because she eliminated the option of doing direct comparison with the counting bags, some of her students began to try alternative methods to compare two quantities. Ricardo and Eliza both solved the problem in a decontextualized form. Granted, they still used counting strategies, but their thinking was in the realm of numbers rather than physical objects. They also had an opportunity to share their thinking with their peers, some of whom will most likely try their strategies in the near future.

Ms. Hildago never put a value on any of the approaches students used. This creates a climate where students are welcome to use whichever strategy makes sense to them. Students who need to see the direct comparison are welcome to replicate the counting bags (which supports their counting and contextualization). Those students who want to try to think about it numerically are welcome to do so and have the support of number lines and charts. In either case, students are learning to connect numbers to quantities and developing a rich number sense as a result.

Expanding Students' Understanding

The opening sentence describing MP2 says, "Mathematically proficient students make sense of quantities *and their relationships in problem situations.*" In addition to building an understanding of quantities, as illustrated above, students need to understand how quantities relate to each other in problems. That means young students need opportunities to develop conceptual understandings of the operations (addition and subtraction) as well as the common mathematical symbols they'll encounter ($+$, $-$, $=$, and so on).

The symbols describe the mathematical relationship between the quantities and are not just commands to perform specific actions. Sometimes workbooks or worksheets for students will offer tips that say, "When you see $+$, you add the numbers" or "When you see $-$, you take away the bottom number." This mentality encourages an autopilot approach to math where students automatically perform basic calculations without thinking or reasoning. We don't want to elicit an automatic response in students based on which symbols they see but want instead to encourage them to consider the values and symbols in connection with one another.

Consider the following example from a second-grade class I observed where students worked on standard addition problems with unknown sums. The teacher made the last example on their page of problems a missing-addend situation ($12 + \_\_ = 25$) to see what her students would do. Much to her surprise, seven out of the twenty students wrote *37* in the blank. This is an example of students not considering the relationship between the values and the symbols. Instead they saw the addition sign as a call to combine the quantities.

MP2 requires that students see a raw number problem as more than just arithmetic with which to perform a specific procedure. Consider the differences in the responses from these second graders from two different classes when asked what 23 + 13 meant.

Making Sense of 23 + 13: Interviews with Two Second-Grade Students

Chelsea

Teacher: What does this mean? (Shows 23 + 13 = on the whiteboard.)

Chelsea: It's an adding problem.

Teacher: Yes, it is. Can you describe what each part of this problem means? Pretend you had to describe this to someone who had never had a math class before. What would you say?

Chelsea: Well . . . the plus sign means you have to add these numbers together, and the equal sign means to put your answer next to it.

Carl

Teacher: I want you to pretend you have to describe what this problem (shows 23 + 13 = on the whiteboard) means to someone who's never had a math class before. What would you say?

Carl: Hmm. I would tell them that these two numbers were things they had, like stickers. And the plus sign means you have to put those stickers together in a big pile.

Teacher: What about the equal sign?

Carl: That's like saying they're the same. So on one side you have your two piles of stickers and on the other side you have both piles together. They're the same thing.

There is a noticeable difference in how each student sees the problem and interprets what it means. Chelsea sees it more as a prescribed task, whereas Carl sees it as an action of putting things together. Carl even contextualized it. Also, think about how each interprets the equal sign. Chelsea sees it more as an identifier showing where to put the answer, whereas Carl sees it as conveying equivalence.

If students are going to reason abstractly and quantitatively, they need to have the kind of understanding Carl exhibits. This comes from K–2 teachers repeatedly giving their students opportunities to make sense of the operations and mathematical symbols. They need lots of practice interpreting contextualized problems so they see the operations as actions that exist in the real world. They also need opportunities to contextualize abstract problems so they can consider and represent the relationships between the values and the symbols. Here are some ways we can do that:

- Give students a raw number problem like 16 – 7 and ask them to create stories, images, or representations that show the expression.
- Give students story problems and ask them to write the equation that represents the mathematics in the problem.
- Ask students to label their visual representations with numbers.
- Ask students to create contexts for problems.
- Facilitate conversations with students that encourage them to move between concrete examples and abstract reasoning.

Following is an example of this work from a first-grade classroom. Ms. Mahoney is working to help her students make sense of operations by connecting them to contextualized story problems. Before you read the vignette, think about the first sentence in MP2 again: "Mathematically proficient students make sense of quantities *and their relationships in problem situations.*" As you read what Ms. Mahoney does, consider how this work supports students in making sense of quantities and their relationships in problem situations.

|| Focus Questions

1. How does this activity support MP2?
2. What other questions could you use with Ms. Mahoney's story?
3. What prior experiences do students need in order to fully access the potential of this activity?

What's My Question?

Ms. Mahoney—Grade 1, March

An activity I like to do with my first graders during our morning meeting is called *What's My Question?* I write a story problem on the Smartboard but leave off the question. I then ask students to come up with possible questions that would work for the context I presented. It's a great way for them to see how the question can completely change the relationship between the values in the problem. It also helps them understand what the operations mean, because we explicitly talk about how the question changes the story, what we're trying to find out, and the methods we're going to use to solve it.

On this particular day I wrote the following sentence on the board: *Our physical education teacher, Mr. Wood, bought 12 red mats and 7 green mats from the store.* After our regular morning meeting routine, I asked kids to come up with possible questions for my story problem.

Nicky: How many mats does he have?

June: How many more red mats does he have?

I wasn't surprised by June's response here. She had been thinking a lot about difference with subtraction and was one of the few in the class who seemed to be thinking about subtraction differently.

Taylor: If he wanted to give away 7 green mats... uh... I want it to be a take-away, but if I take away the green mats, it's just 12. That's not right.

Teacher: What's not right?

Taylor: Twelve minus 7 is 5, but I can't do 12 minus 7 here because it's 12. That's weird. I don't get it.

Silvana: It's 19 minus 7. The mats are together.

Taylor: Ohhhh. But then how do I make it 12 minus 7?

Silvana: That's wrong because it's 19 mats. It's not 12.

Teacher: Well, let's see if we can make it work. What story would make us have 12 minus 7?

June: Mine does! You can do 12 minus 7 to know how many more red mats he has.

Teacher: You knew that when we compare two numbers, that's a kind of subtraction. Does that work for you, Taylor?

Taylor: I guess. I was just trying to get Mr. Wood to give away mats. You know... take away.

Teacher: I think we can make that work. Can we use cubes to see what's making this tricky? (Taylor gets 12 red cubes and 7 green cubes.) What's happening?

Taylor: I want to do 12 take away 7, but it's 19 altogether.

Devon: I got it! What if he has to give away a red mat with the green mats?

Silvana: That's 19 minus 7 minus 7.

Teacher: These are great ideas. Remember how our story can change how we think about the problem? Can we come up with a story that would work for Taylor's idea?

Devon: Mr. Wood . . . has to give . . . has to have a red and green mat for Battleship (a game they play with mats).

Taylor: He needs 7 red and green mats.

Devon: Yeah, Mr. Wood needs 7 red and green mats for Battleship. How many red mats does he have left? (High-fives Taylor.)

Teacher: That seems to work. Now I want you to work in pairs and choose a question to answer. Remember, you have to write the equation or number sentence (I pair the math language with the kid language) and create a picture or representation to show how you solved it.

Ms. Mahoney's *What's My Question?* routine is a very powerful activity. MP2 is about helping students understand the values in problems and how they relate to one another. Students need to learn to put numerical representations into contexts as well as how to decontextualize a story situation. This activity supports all of that work in a very effective way. Students are given a context around certain values in a given situation—in this case, the number of mats of a specific color. As presented, there is no reason to operate with 7 and 12 or consider what relationship to use. However, once students have to design a question, the values have significance.

For students to design effective questions, they have to contextualize the relationship they want to convey. Nicky thought of the problem as an accumulation of mats and asked the question, "How many does he have now?" That question meant that the two values were addends in an addition situation and needed to be combined. June thought of it as a comparison situation and asked the question, "How many more red mats does he have?" That made the red and green mats distinct values that needed to be compared, and she did that by subtracting. As students debated specific questions, they were continually thinking about the meaning of the operations and the relationship between the values in the problem.

Ms. Mahoney's students had lots of experience solving contextualized tasks. Many of these tasks were in the form of word problems, but others were based on situations in the classroom or were connected to math games students played. This prior experience of exploring a variety of contexts paved the way for students to really be successful with this task of creating questions for contextualized situations. They were able to access their prior knowledge and experience with previous problem structures and questions to devise their own.

Support Students' Mathematical Reasoning

In the last section of MP2 it says, "Quantitative reasoning entails habits of creating a coherent representation of the problem at hand; considering the units involved; attending to the meaning of quantities, not just how to compute them; and knowing and flexibly using different properties of operations and objects."   In essence, kids should approach problems thoughtfully and flexibly.

Quantitative reasoning is a skill that students develop over time when given ample opportunities to think about numbers and operations in meaningful ways. One way to ensure you are supporting quantitative reasoning is to allow students to use their own approaches to solve problems. If the expectation is that there is one preferred procedure for solving any given task, students will focus only on that approach. Remember the example of a student solving 12 + 15 using a context of pencils coming in boxes of 10? What if the teacher required her students to use a structure that promoted the standard algorithm instead of their own reasoning to solve the problem? (See Figure 2.5 compared to Figure 2.6.)

Tens	Ones
1	2
1	5
2	7

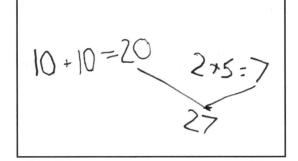

Figure 2.5 Structure for algorithm   Figure 2.6 Numerical reasoning

If students were only required to plug numbers into a structure that was presented to them, the rich mathematical reasoning they shared would not have surfaced. Instead, they would have walked through the steps without having to think much at all. In the first example, the student added single digits in columns. When asked to explain, he said, "Two plus 5 is 7. And 1 plus 1 is 2 so it's 27." When asked how it makes 27 the student said, "I don't know ... because the 2 and the 7 are next to each other?" Although he could compute and get the correct answer with the structure presented to him, he didn't have a strong understanding of place value and couldn't explain why adding that way worked.

In the second example the student thought about boxes of pencils that come in packs of 10. She added the numbers using a place-value strategy that made sense to her and combined the partial sums to get her answer. She had ownership of the whole process and her strategy was efficient and made sense to her. Mathematically, both approaches were similar, but only the second one involved a student using quantitative reasoning.

When we allow our students to approach problems in ways that make sense to them, they will develop conceptual understandings of numbers, operations, and the base ten structure of our number system. These understandings are necessary if students are to learn to reason abstractly and quantitatively. They will learn to naturally contextualize situations by using manipulatives to act out the actions of the operations. They will see the relationships between the quantities involved because they created meaningful representations. Throughout this work, some students will be more efficient than others. Our job is to help each student see how his or her individual approach connects to the others so they develop flexible and efficient problem-solving strategies.

When we encourage students to use strategies that make sense to them, we allow them to work at a level that is developmentally appropriate. Many kindergartners and first graders directly model problems in order to solve them. It makes sense when you consider they are just beginning to develop an understanding of numbers, quantity, base ten, and so on. When they are presented with a problem such as "Megan saw 5 birds in her garden and 6 birds in the birdbath. How many birds did she see?" some will naturally solve it by drawing 5 birds in a garden and 6 birds in a birdbath and then counting them all to get 11. (See Figure 2.7.)

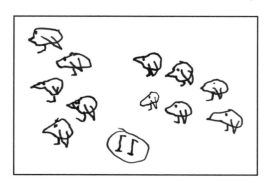

Figure 2.7 Solution using detailed pictures

Young students need to see both numbers represented, because most are still developing their sense of quantity. Although drawing both quantities and counting them is an inefficient approach for older students, it is necessary for primary-grade students if we want them to learn to attend to the meaning of the quantities, create coherent representations of problems, and consider the units involved. As they mature, we can support students in becoming more efficient by encouraging them to create simplified pictures instead of detailed artistic ones. (See Figure 2.8.)

Over time, as students develop stronger understandings of numbers and operations, their strategies will evolve and become more efficient. They will begin to hold on to one quantity and count on or back to solve problems. (See Figure 2.9.)

Figure 2.8 Solution using simplified pictures

This strategy evolves from the "count-all" approach in which all values are represented with pictures or objects, and is rooted in students' understanding of quantity. When students reach this point, they no longer need to represent the starting quantity because they understand that the number 5 is the same as 5 objects. They no longer need to count the first set to count on with the second set. As with the direct modeling approach, the counting-on or -back approach supports students as they attend to the meaning of the quantities, create coherent representations of the problem, and consider the units involved.

Figure 2.9 Solution using a count-on method

During students' experiences as they progress from kindergarten through second grade, they continually deepen their number sense and understanding of operations and the base ten structure of our number system. Throughout this process, they will begin to use numerical reasoning when their understanding allows for it. In the case of the bird problem, a first grader might recall a math fact he or she has mastered and say, "I know that 5 plus 5 equals 10 so one more is 11." Other students might think about a ten-frame structure. In this case, they visualize a frame of 5 and a frame of 6 and see the 6 as a row of 5 with one extra (see Figure 2.10). By combining the two rows of 5, they fill a frame of 10 and have one extra to make 11 (see Figure 2.11).

If we want our students to reason abstractly and quantitatively; have flexible strategies to solve problems in ways that make sense; and attend to the meaning of the quantities, create coherent representations of the problem, and consider the units involved, then we need to allow them to develop and use strategies that are grounded in their understanding and make sense to them. If we rush them through the process in an effort to get them to use a shortcut or specific procedure, they will

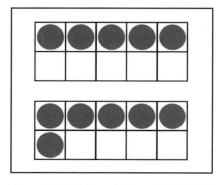 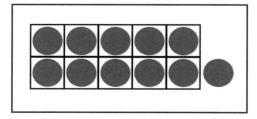

Figure 2.10 (Left) and **Figure 2.11** (Right) Solution using a ten-frame

miss out on all the rich opportunities to make sense of math and will instead rely on tricks and procedures that don't have any meaning for them (Wu and Lin 2016).

MP2 supports students as they learn to approach problem solving as a thoughtful process. They learn to connect mathematics to contextualized situations and develop flexible and efficient methods for solving them. We support our students in this endeavor by helping them attend to the meanings of quantities, symbols, and operations. The math world can become very intuitive when students are given a chance to experience it in ways that are connected to contexts and experiences that make sense. Our job is to make that happen on a daily basis.

This was a huge pedagogical shift for me when I began teaching, because I used to see my role as the instructor who showed students how to do math. Over time, I developed a better understanding of the various ways in which my second graders made sense of mathematical ideas. I engaged in more professional learning to help me understand how to facilitate learning rather than dictate it. I learned more about the cognitive abilities of seven- and eight-year-olds, which gave me a better sense of what was reasonable to expect of them at any given point in the school year. Finally, I learned to really focus on each student to get a sense of what they knew and how they learned so I could use that information to best meet their needs.

As you reflect on your own practice, consider where you are with your own mathematical content and pedagogical knowledge as it relates to reasoning abstractly and quantitatively. Which areas do you need to develop in terms of your own understanding? Were there sections in this chapter that seemed less familiar than others? Were there teacher moves in the vignettes that were new to you? These kinds of reflections can help you develop a plan for your own professional learning and help you think about shifts you may need to make to fully support the development of MP2 in your classroom.

CHAPTER 3

Mathematical Practice 3: Construct Viable Arguments and Critique the Reasoning of Others

Think of a time when you really had to make a case for something. Perhaps it was a new purchase you wanted to make, a decision about where to take a family vacation, or an idea you had for a professional learning community in your school. Regardless of the particular scenario, I'd like you to think about the preparation you did before presenting your case and what considerations you took into account about how to present your argument.

When I wanted to rent a booth at the National Council of Supervisors of Mathematics annual meeting to highlight our Summer Math Institutes and Master of Arts in Mathematics Teaching program at Mount Holyoke College, I had to present a case to our financial analyst for approval. Having never created an exhibition booth or worked at one, I had to do a lot of research to understand all the components involved. When I eventually presented my arguments, I chose to do so with the aid of graphs, tables, charts, photographs, and a compelling narrative, because I thought they would help provide a clearer picture of what I hoped to accomplish.

Although I thought I had done a thorough job, our analyst had a slew of questions I hadn't anticipated. My argument had holes in it that had to be filled. I went back to my office and worked to find the answers he needed. Shortly afterward, I presented a new case with updated charts and more data and helped convince him that this was a worthy investment.

MP3: "Construct Viable Arguments and Critique the Reasoning of Others" is very similar to what transpired at my office. It comes down to justification. I needed to justify why I wanted to invest money in a booth, and to do so, I used materials at my disposal to help clarify my points so others could make sense of them. My colleague, in turn, critiqued my justifications and asked questions that pointed out the holes in my argument. This helped me revise my thinking and develop a much more comprehensive argument for my cause.

The same is true in our math classrooms. We want our students to construct mathematical arguments for a variety of purposes: to explain their reasoning behind a particular strategy or approach to a mathematical task, to justify their answer to a problem, to prove why a conjecture they made is true or to disprove another conjecture, and to communicate their mathematical thinking to their peers and teachers. Students are also expected to think critically about the arguments put forth by their peers to see if they hold true or need to be revised. They are encouraged to ask questions about their classmates' thinking to get clarification or to point out areas of disagreement in an effort to collectively work toward greater understanding.

Working on MP3 promotes productive and active mathematical discourse in the classroom and encourages students to talk about their ideas, make and test conjectures, and have open debate about particular strategies or ideas. This kind of communication makes up the essence of what it means to do mathematics (Stein 2007). Rather than work in an insular manner in which thinking is shared only between individual students and their teacher, students today should share ideas with one another so they can collectively build a greater understanding.

Creating a classroom culture where productive mathematical discourse is the norm takes time to establish. You will have to spend time establishing the expectations for what it means to engage in mathematical discourse and provide ample opportunities for students to practice this skill. Creating a set of classroom norms may help students understand their role in math talks and ensure that your energy is spent on facilitating the discussion rather than managing behavior. The norms in Figure 3.1 are from the last second-grade class I taught.

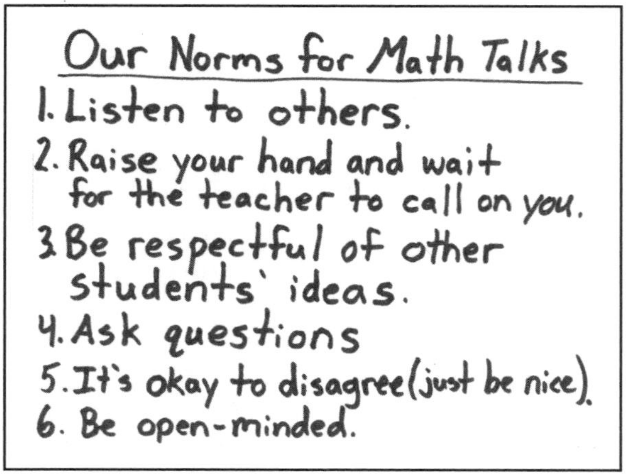

We established the first four in the beginning of the year, and they are pretty much standard in most classrooms. The others

Our Norms for Math Talks
1. Listen to others.
2. Raise your hand and wait for the teacher to call on you.
3. Be respectful of other students' ideas.
4. Ask questions
5. It's okay to disagree (just be nice).
6. Be open-minded.

Figure 3.1 Classroom norms

were added when issues came up. For example, when students critiqued each other for the first time, we had some hurt feelings because of a few terse comments from peers. We debriefed about it and then added number 5 to the list. Number 6 was added when I noticed students were quick to dismiss ideas because they were fixated on their own thinking.

Having norms like these posted in the room provides an easy reference for students so they understand some general rules for constructing arguments and critiquing the reasoning of others. I know some teachers who go a step further and provide anchor charts with sentence frames that model how to critique others respectfully. Here are some examples:

- "I disagree with _____ because I think _____."
- "My thinking is different from _____ because _____."
- I like how _____ said _____, but I think _____."

I never used sentence frames with my second graders, but I have seen them used very effectively in K–2 classrooms. Teachers used them to teach students how they might critique others in a respectful way, but eventually took them off the wall to help promote more natural discussions. Relying solely on sentence frames can make discussions sound stilted and unnatural, but they are helpful if students have no sense of how to engage in a debate about a mathematical idea.

Taking the time early in the school year to establish this culture of promoting mathematical discourse will help set the stage to support MP3. If students don't know how to talk about their own thinking or how to listen to the thinking of others, then constructing arguments and critiquing the reasoning of others will be difficult for them. For students in the primary grades, learning to do things such as sit quietly and look at the person who is talking is a fairly new skill and takes time to develop. These skills are just as important to establish as learning to use representations to support a mathematical argument. When working to teach the MPs, K–2 teachers have the added challenge of teaching and reinforcing a myriad of skills and behaviors that support this work.

Additionally, we must consider the kind of mathematics classroom that is needed to support this work. When I grew up, the closest I ever came to being asked to make a mathematical argument was to show my work on the assigned practice pages. This was really just to prove that I wasn't copying off my neighbor and that I actually worked through the steps my teachers showed me. There was no need for me to create an argument, because there was nothing I needed to justify. I was just doing what the teacher told me to do to get the answers.

Today's math classrooms are very different, because students are expected to develop and refine their own strategies to solve problems and complete tasks. Instead of showing students a procedure for getting an answer and then having them practice that procedure, we give them a problem and ask them to figure out how to solve it. That means students have to make choices. They have to work from their own understanding and devise approaches that make sense to them. It also means that for any given problem or task, there will be a range of ideas from students about how to go about completing it.

When the ideas emerge from the students rather than the teacher, it is important that students be able to justify their reasoning both to themselves and to their peers. This not only provides a window into each student's mathematical reasoning and understanding, but also serves as a vehicle to share new ideas. If we truly want to act as facilitators of learning, we need students to take a very active role in classroom discussions. Learning how to construct viable arguments and critique the reasoning of others is imperative to this cause.

The arguments from students and the math discussions that result from them provide opportunities for teachers to help students solidify and consolidate their thinking and understanding, introduce new ideas for consideration, challenge students' preconceived reasoning, and build a collective understanding. Facilitating such discussions requires teachers to be purposeful in their interactions with students as they work independently or in small groups.

As teachers observe students, they should note the various strategies or ways of thinking about a particular idea. By having a sense of the full range of their students' thinking, teachers can begin to plan and orchestrate a whole-group discussion that not only helps students learn to create and critique mathematical arguments, but also supports the overall understanding of the particular learning objective of the day. Rather than call the students back together toward the end of class and randomly call on volunteers to share their thinking, the teacher has a flexible agenda in her head and some specific students in mind whose ideas she wants brought to the whole group.

I sometimes equate this approach to putting on a play. In this case, the plot is the actual mathematical ideas and goals the teacher wants highlighted as a result of the discussion. She has a rough idea of the kinds of outcomes she is looking for as a result of this work before the lesson even begins. Then as students work independently or in small groups, she moves around the room acting like a casting agent, looking for students who might fill particular roles in the discussion.

For example, if the teacher's goal is to have students draw connections between numerical representations and pictorial representations of problem-solving strategies, she might find a student who used a base ten representation and another student who broke the numbers apart. Then during the whole-class discussion she will make sure these students get a chance to share so other students are able to connect similar strategies using different representations. She may decide to call on the students directly or make it feel more natural by asking students to volunteer but making sure, in the end, to call on those two. In either case, she has an agenda and purposefully chooses specific students to help get those ideas across.

Consider this example from a first-grade classroom where the teacher wanted her students to move toward more efficient strategies for solving addition problems. Rather than show her students a particular approach, she encouraged them to use their own strategies and then facilitated a discussion in which they had to argue why their approach was efficient.

Focus Questions

1. As you follow the flow of the discussion, consider the benefit of structuring the discussion from least efficient to most efficient. How might that help students connect to their peers' ideas?
2. How is the teacher supporting students in making mathematical arguments and critiquing the reasoning of others?

I Counted Really Fast

Ms. Granger—Grade 1, November

During the previous week my students had been working on solving story problems involving addition and justifying their strategies to their peers. Most of my students were using a count-all approach, whereas a few were counting on and one was using a numerical approach. What was surprising to me, though, was the degree to which students were being inefficient in their drawings as they worked to solve the problems.

Obviously one big goal in first grade is for students to eventually develop more efficient strategies for solving problems, but it's also important for them to make sense of the math. If a student needs to count everything in the problem to make sense of it, it would be unreasonable for me to just tell him or her to jump to a count-on or numerical approach because it's faster. Sure, they could probably replicate what I tell them to do, but it wouldn't be based on their understanding.

That said, there are places where students can be more efficient while still working with mathematical ideas that make sense to them. As I said, the bulk of my students are counting all when solving, but a good number of them also draw very specific, detailed drawings. They could be much more efficient if they would simply use tally marks or circles instead of drawing the specific objects from the problem. I decided to push this idea by introducing the students to the word *efficient* and asked them to think about what that means in math. We decided that it meant working on a problem in the best possible way without wasting time. I then asked them to think about how they were being efficient as they worked on the following problem:

> **JENNA PICKED 7 PURPLE FLOWERS ON MONDAY AND 8 RED FLOWERS ON TUESDAY. HOW MANY FLOWERS DID SHE PICK?**

Students went to work, and I observed a wide array of strategies being implemented. As they worked, I walked around, observed what they were doing, and made quick notes about their strategies to help me keep track of their approaches. I created an anecdotal recording grid to make this easier (see Figure 3.2).

	Solves problem with detailed pictures	Solves problem with efficient pictures	Counts objects or fingers	Uses numerical reasoning	Notes
Madison					
Halle					
Emily C.					
Anna					
Delaney					

Figure 3.2 Anecdotal Recording Grid

Across the top I put the approaches I anticipated would arise as a result of this work. I also organized them from least efficient to most efficient to help me gauge where students would fall on this continuum. While I observed students work, I placed a check under the strategies they used and added some notes in the last sections.

During this session, some students got out crayons and chose purple and red to draw the flowers. One group got cubes and picked out 7 purple cubes and 8 red ones. Another group used cubes but didn't bother coordinating colors. They grabbed 7 random cubes and then 8 random cubes and counted them all together. Two students used tally marks, and two students drew flowers with pencils. I did see a few students count on from 7 using their fingers, and a few counted on from 7 using tally marks. One student counted on from 8 with tally marks. Finally, one student used numerical reasoning, saying that $7 + 7 = 14$ and 1 more is 15.

I called the group together and asked students to share their strategies and to tell us how they were being efficient. I wanted the students to not only describe and justify their strategies, but articulate why they thought their approach was efficient. Constructing viable arguments is a new concept for first graders, and I wanted them to get lots of practice doing it. I chose students in order from the least efficient approaches to the most efficient so the ideas could build. Each student placed his or her work under the document camera as he or she shared so the class could see their thinking.

Sasha: I got 15. I drew 7 purples here and 8 red ones. Then I went (pointing to each flower as she counts) 1, 2, 3, 4, 5, 6, 7, 8, 9, 10, 11, 12, 13, 14, 15.

Teacher: And can you tell us how you were working to be more efficient?

Sasha: I counted really fast.

I stifled a laugh. In trying to define efficiency, I think I might have overemphasized speed. I didn't want to dwell on it because this discussion was really about students making mathematical arguments. I decided to clarify briefly but move on to the main point of the discussion.

Teacher: That's good, Sasha. Who else solved it like Sasha by drawing flowers and counting them all? (Six more hands are raised.) I noticed many of you counting very fast like Sasha said. I just want to say one thing about that. Being efficient sometimes means doing things at a fast pace, but it doesn't always mean we have to work extra fast. And sometimes when we count too fast, we make mistakes, so we just want to be careful about that. Being efficient also means solving problems with fewer steps so it doesn't take as long. Did anyone have another way to be efficient? (Although lots of hands are up, I am waiting for specific hands so I can call on students in a particular order.) Tricia?

Tricia: I think mine was 'ficient 'cause I used cubes.

Teacher: How did cubes help you be more efficient?

Tricia: I draw slow, and it's quicker to count cubes 'cause they're already there. You don't have to make them.

Teacher (to the class): What do you all think about that?

Aiden: Only if you draw flowers.

Teacher: What do you mean?

Aiden: You can just draw circles or squares or Xs. You don't have to actually draw flowers.

Teacher: So making simpler drawings is a way to be more efficient? (Heads nod.) Okay. What do you think about that, Tricia?

Tricia: Um . . . Maybe with just a few, but not if there were a lot of them. Your hand would get tired. You would have to draw slow and need rest. I just like counting cubes. It's fast for me.

Aiden: Drawing's fast for me. I don't get tired.

Teacher: You each seemed to find a way that works for you. That's good. (To the class.) Any other thoughts on drawing things like circles or squares versus using cubes? (No response.) Okay, who has another way? (Again, hands go up, but I wait for Julian because I want him to share next.)

Julian: I kinda did it like Aiden, but different. I did lines like this. (He shows his paper, which has the number 7 with a circle around it followed by 8 lines.) It's faster because you only have to make 8 lines. (See Figure 3.3.)

Figure 3.3 Julian's strategy

Ronjit: That's what I did except I put 8 in my head instead of 7 and I went like this (begins counting on his fingers): 9, 10, 11, 12, 13, 14, 15.

Teacher: And how is that more efficient?

Ronjit: I only needed 7 lines. It doesn't matter here, but if it was like a hundred plus . . . say . . . 4. You don't want to do a hundred lines so you go 100 (counts on fingers) 101, 102, 103, 104. Yeah.

Teacher: Starting with a bigger number in your head is more efficient?

Ronjit: Yeah. You don't have to make as many lines.

Teacher: What do others think about this statement about Ronjit's idea?

Sandy: I like it.

Teacher: What do you like about it?

Sandy: Kinda like what he said. You don't have to make as many things after it . . . like lines or stars or whatever.

Teacher: We have a lot of ways that we're being efficient. Bella, you have been very patient. Do you want to share your way?

Bella: I just said 7 plus 7 equals 14 so 1 more is 15.

Teacher: Why did you start with 7 plus 7?

Bella: Because I already know that one.

Teacher: So you used a combination you already knew to solve a new one? (She nods.) Can you tell us how that helps you be efficient?

Bella: It's like I already know the answer. I just go 14 and then say 15. It's like a few seconds long.

At this point I decided to start listing these approaches on a continuum on chart paper so students could see what they identified in terms of efficiency. From left to right it read, "Count all with pictures, count all with lines, count all with cubes, count on starting with smaller number, count on starting with bigger number, using a combination we know."

Teacher: These are all the different ways we've been efficient today. Some of you noticed that some ways are more efficient than others, and some of you may have discovered new ways you can be more efficient when trying to solve problems. I'm going to post this list on the wall and ask that you think about your strategy and then think of a way you might be more efficient when we work on more problems tomorrow.

Clearly, Ms. Granger was very mindful of the nuances involved as she worked to orchestrate a math discussion emphasizing students' mathematical arguments. Her overarching goal was to help her students become more efficient problem solvers, but she allowed the work to originate with them rather than her. This approach achieved a number of outcomes. First, each student was able to work from his or her own place of understanding. Students chose strategies that made sense to them, and Ms. Granger accepted and valued each one. Another outcome was that each student who shared had to justify to the rest of the class why his or her approach was efficient. The other students also had opportunities to ask questions and critique the reasoning of others.

Ms. Granger's questioning and clarifying helped support students in making mathematical arguments. She asked each student to explain his or her strategy and how the approach was efficient. Students had to do this in their own words and she refrained from restating what they said. She then invited the others to comment and critique the statement. When Tricia argued that using cubes was faster than drawing, Ms. Granger asked, "What do you all think about that?" This move opened up the floor for others to critique Tricia's reasoning. Once Aiden responded, she asked Tricia to comment on his critique, allowing for a bit of back and forth between the two students. Teachers have an extremely important role in facilitating strong math discussions (Kazemi and Hintz 2014). Ms. Granger asked many open-ended questions that allowed for more talk on the students' part, and carefully listened to their statements. She then asked clarifying follow-up questions to help students be more precise. From the students' perspective, it seemed like the ideas and conversation are all coming from them and that their teacher was just working to understand all the different ideas they were sharing. This ownership is key in creating math talks in which students are invested.

Notice too the intentionality of Ms. Granger's choice of students to share their thinking. She wanted the ideas to progress from the least efficient to the most efficient, and she chose students accordingly. Although she selected the students during their work time, she never revealed that during the discussion. Rather than call down the list of names she chose, she purposefully made the discussion seem organic by asking all students if they had a more efficient approach. This caused all students to consider their own thinking before she chose the particular student she wanted to share next.

The intention to call kids in order based on levels of efficiency also served a purpose. By starting with the least efficient, she ensured that the maximum range of responses would come up and more students would have to make mathematical arguments. Her students' strategies fell on a continuum, with some students using very inefficient, count-all approaches all the way to one student using numerical reasoning. This continuum seemed to develop naturally as part of the conversation and Ms. Granger was able to use it to help students see where they fell on it and where each student should be going next. It also can serve as a reference point for future arguments as students can refer to it when justifying their strategies in future discussions.

Ms. Granger's vignette demonstrates the power in having students justify their own reasoning. This communicates to students that they should be purposeful in their approaches to mathematical tasks. We want our students thinking about their intent when they choose one strategy or approach instead of just plugging away to get answers. Expecting them to construct viable arguments communicates that their mathematical ideas are important, not only for them, but also for their classmates and for their teachers. It also solidifies the point that mathematical ideas develop and build as a result of our collective work and thinking rather than individual achievement.

If we want our students to construct mathematical arguments and critique the reasoning of others, we need to create a culture where that is the norm in math class. The foundation for this work begins in kindergarten as students first experience formal math lessons. What's nice about this time is that students aren't coming with deeply rooted, preconceived notions of what math class should look and sound like. The expectations we set form the basis for their understanding of their role in the classroom. If we start in kindergarten with the expectation that students are active participants in all parts of a math lesson, then that becomes their paradigm for what it means to be a math student. They also learn how to be a responsible group participant, which is another foundational skill.

One simple way to achieve this is to question students frequently about their motivations and intentions. Each time a student has to justify her thinking, she is constructing mathematical arguments. If this kind of questioning is a regular part of math class, students very quickly learn that they have to be purposeful in their work because they may have to defend the choices they make. The key is to ask open-ended questions that elicit student thinking. Here are some examples:

- Why did you use _____ to help you with this task?
- How do you know this was the best approach?
- Do you think that pattern works for all shapes? How do you know?
- Why does that answer not make sense?
- Why does that make sense to you?
- Why was that the most efficient approach?

Each of these questions puts the onus on the students to describe what they did and why they did it. Teachers can ask these kinds of questions of individuals as they work independently or of partners or teams as they work together. They can also be used when facilitating whole-group discussions. This kind of questioning can begin as early as kindergarten and provide many opportunities for students to justify their reasoning to others.

How our students present their arguments is also important. Although arguments often are quickly verbalized, students can support their arguments with concrete referents like drawings, cube models, diagrams, tables, charts, and number lines, as well as actions on those referents (for example, joining cubes together to show the action of addition or removing cubes to show the action of subtraction). These help convey a student's argument and make it easier for others to understand. They also provide a point of reference for others to comment and critique during a discussion.

Using concrete referents is particularly helpful in the primary grades because young students are still developing their mathematical vocabulary. Having a model to manipulate helps young students convey a mathematical idea that they cannot yet communicate verbally. For example, consider how Daisy, a kindergartner, manipulated the shapes in Figure 3.4 to convey their congruency and make an argument that they were the same without knowing the correct terminology.

Daisy: You can see it. You just twist them and they match.

Although young students are just beginning to learn how to communicate their mathematical thinking, they can still begin constructing viable arguments and critiquing the reasoning of others. Consider the following example in which kindergartners describe how they covered a shape with the pattern blocks.

Figure 3.4 Congruent shapes

Focus Questions

1. How are the students using concrete referents to help make their arguments?
2. How does the teacher support kindergartners in making mathematical arguments and critiquing the reasoning of others?

Brown Is Skinny and Green Is Fat

Ms. Morrissey—Kindergarten, December

I have been working with my kindergartners for a while now on talking about their math work with their partners and with the class. They have been practicing using their words to say what they did and using pictures or manipulatives to help them explain their thinking to their classmates. For this particular task, the students were instructed to fill in a shape that looked like a cat. They could use any blocks they wanted, but I let them know that the final covered shape should still look like the original pattern. I also asked them to count the total number of blocks they used.

When they came to the floor for the discussion, their task was to explain what they had done so others could understand how they filled in the shape. Most students filled in the shape following the exact outline. They used one hexagon, two trapezoids, two triangles, and one tan rhombus. (See Figure 3.5.)

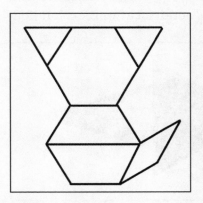

Figure 3.5 Original cat outline

However, Trina was one of the few who tried using all triangles. After a few students shared how they filled it in with six blocks, I asked Trina to share.

Trina: I used a lot of blocks. I got sixteen.

Teacher: Wow, sixteen does sound like a lot of blocks. Can you show us how you fit sixteen blocks on the picture?

Trina: I used all these (holds up a few triangles).

Teacher: You used triangles? Can you show us how you did it?

Trina: I went like this (starts placing triangles on the sheet as shown in Figure 3.6).

Teacher: Trina, can you tell us why you chose triangles?

Trina: 'Cause they're the smallest. I can fit more in here. Like . . . you can't use yellows (referring to the yellow hexagons) . . . they're too big.

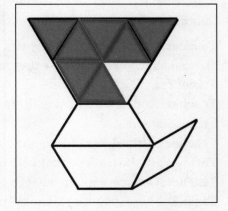

Figure 3.6 Trina's initial covering of the cat outline

Tariq: Yes you can. In the middle.

Trina: Not on the whole thing! Triangles fit all over. They're the teeniest. (See Figure 3.7.)

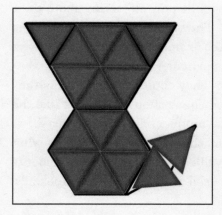

Figure 3.7 Trina's completed covering of the cat outline

Autumn: Triangles aren't the teeniest. The brown ones are the teeniest.

Teacher: Why do you say that?

Autumn: See? Brown is skinny and green is fat, see? (She holds them up next to each other as shown in Figure 3.8.)

Trina: Yeah, but look at it sticking out (pointing to the tan rhombus). That's bigger.

Autumn: Oops.

At this moment, I did not choose to explore whether the triangle was bigger than the thin rhombus, but I did note it for a future exploration, because it would provide a great opportunity for my kindergartners to practice making arguments. I refocused the girls on our math talk. I was curious whether anyone would call out the fact that Trina covered the tail part of the picture with two triangles even though they didn't fit.

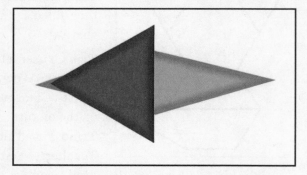

Figure 3.8 Triangle and rhombus comparison

Teacher: Trina, you say that you used all triangles because they were the smallest block?

Trina: Yes.

Teacher: And how many was that?

Trina: Sixteen.

Teacher to the class: Did anyone else get sixteen or more than sixteen?

Tariq: Wait, she can't do that with the tail. It's only a tan one.

Teacher: Can you explain what you mean?

Tariq: See here (pointing to the tail part of the picture), it's only a tan one. (He removes two triangles and replaces them with a tan rhombus as shown in Figure 3.9.)

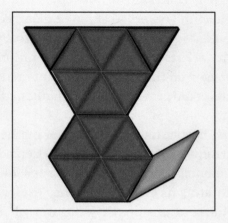

Figure 3.9 Tariq's correction

Teacher: If you do that, how many blocks are there?

Tariq: Fifteen.

Teacher: Trina, what do you think about Tariq's idea that triangles don't fit on the tail?

Trina: (Shrugs.) I don't know.

Teacher: Do you think triangles fit here?

Trina: Well . . . you can't see the lines.

Tariq: They don't look the same. See? (Puts the papers side by side as shown in Figures 3.10 and 3.11.) Hers is bigger.

Trina: Oh yeah.

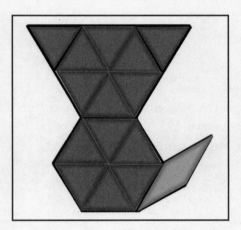

Figure 3.10 Tariq's version

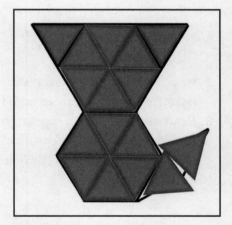

Figure 3.11 Trina's version

This exchange demonstrates how young students use a combination of oral language and concrete referents to construct arguments and critique others' reasoning. Although Autumn wasn't able to use words to describe that the tan rhombus was smaller than the triangle, she was able to *demonstrate* her point using the actual blocks. Trina then used that same visual to make a counterargument that the tan was bigger because the piece was sticking out. The concrete referents provided an anchor point that helped both students convey their arguments.

As with the first-grade vignette, the teacher here asked a lot of questions requiring students to justify their thinking and welcoming others to agree or disagree. The ownership of the thinking lay with the students while the teacher masterfully asked the right questions and provided the right tasks to encourage argumentation. She also made sure to keep the discussion focused on the original task, but made note of a possible future activity where students could practice making mathematical arguments about which shape was bigger.

As students get older, they begin developing deeper understandings of mathematical concepts, and their arguments and critiques become more sophisticated. Students become more adept at conversing amongst themselves so the teacher doesn't have to handhold as much while facilitating discussions. As they explore things such as the behaviors of operations or the relationships they discover when working with shapes, students will make conjectures and work to prove or disprove them. In this final vignette, we'll see second graders creating mathematical arguments about which half of a sandwich is bigger.

Focus Questions

1. How does this particular task lend itself to encouraging students to construct viable arguments and critique the reasoning of others?
2. How does the teacher work to support this work?
3. How does the collective work of the students contribute to an overall understanding of the equivalence of the two shapes?

Triangles Are More 'Cause They're Bigger!

Ms. Perch—Grade 2, February

As a way to introduce my students to the concept of half, I cut several sheets of paper into 8-by-8-inch squares and handed them out. I told students that the squares were sandwiches and that they needed to share their sandwich equally with a friend. The students immediately began folding and cutting their squares in one of two ways. Some folded the paper lengthwise, whereas others folded diagonally (see Figure 3.12). In a short amount of time, every student had either rectangles or triangles on their tables, and all agreed that they had shared their sandwich equally.

I then held up one rectangle half and one triangle half and asked if they were each half of a sandwich. The class all agreed that they were. I then said, "If each of these

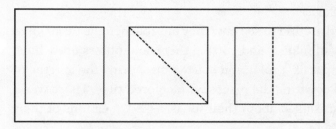

Figure 3.12 Sandwich cuts

shapes is half of a sandwich, are these two shapes equal?" (See Figure 3.13.)

This stirred a lot of debate among the students.

Nora: No, the triangle is bigger.

Zak: Yeah. (Takes both shapes and overlaps them as shown in Figure 3.14.) You can see the point sticking out.

Jeslyn: I think they are the same.

Teacher: So you think they're equal?

Jeslyn: Yes . . . I think. They'd have to be, but I . . . I'm not sure how to say it.

Teacher: Give it a try. Why do you think they'd have to be?

Jeslyn: 'Cause they came from the same square. Well, not the same one, but all the sandwiches were the same size.

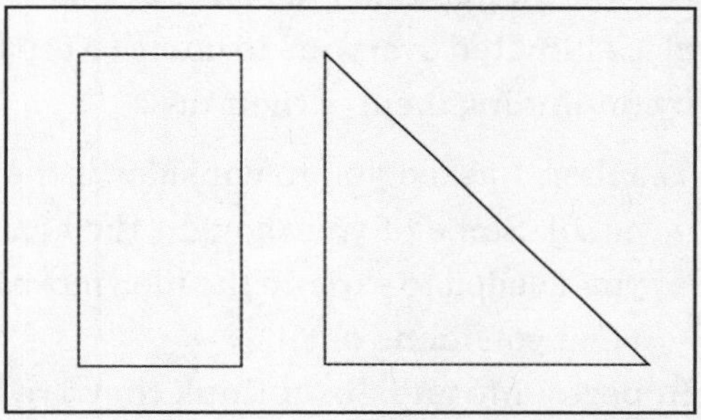

Harrison: I think the triangle is bigger.

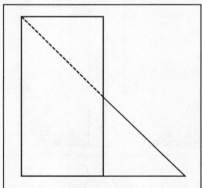

Figure 3.13 Triangle and rectangle comparison

Edith: So if you cut the sandwich into triangles, the halves give you more?

Harrison: Yeah. Triangles are more, 'cause they're bigger.

Edith: That doesn't make sense.

Teacher: What doesn't make sense?

Edith: It shouldn't matter how you cut it. They're still the same.

Teacher: This is great! We have a lot of good ideas going around. Some think the pieces are equal and some think they're not. And it looks like some aren't sure yet. Here's what we're going to do. I want you to work with your partners to either prove they are equal or prove they are not, depending on what you think. If you aren't sure yet, use this time to see if you can figure it out.

Figure 3.14 Overlap of the two shapes

Harrison: Can we cut more shapes?

Teacher: I'd like you to do what you need to do to figure this out and have an argument ready to present at the end of class.

I set them to work and walked around to see how they approached the task. Some grabbed lots of squares and began folding and cutting them, and others drew lines to indicate cut marks. One group took a ruler and started measuring the lengths of the pieces. Another group tried covering the pieces with colored tiles. There was a lot of chatter in the room as kids talked about their ideas, asked questions of their partners, and revised their thinking.

I mostly monitored the conversations and occasionally asked clarifying questions when students offered their explanations. I didn't want to interject too much, because I wanted them to construct their own arguments. With fifteen minutes left in class I invited everyone to come to the meeting area to share their thinking. I began by reminding them of their task.

Teacher: I asked you to consider if the triangle piece and the rectangle piece were equal. Some of you thought they were, some thought they weren't, and some of you needed to explore the idea more before making up your minds. Now let's hear what you found out.

Roberto: Me and Soshi think they are because if you fold them like . . . well, if you fold the triangle like this (lays the rectangle on top of the triangle so the lengths match and then wraps the piece that sticks out from the triangle back onto the rectangle), you see? It still matches and makes a rectangle. (See Figure 3.15.)

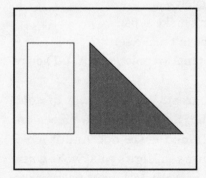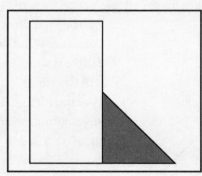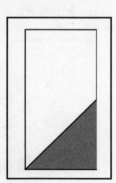

Figure 3.15 a,b,c Roberto and Soshi's representation

Mackenzie, furrowing her brow: Yeah, but that triangle is still extra.

Teacher: Which triangle?

Mackenzie: The one they folded over. It makes the rectangle, but that little triangle is still extra. You have to count it.

Harrison: Yeah. Like if you cut it. You cut it off. If you just stick it on the rectangle, it's extra—even if you hide it in the rectangle.

Teacher: So you're saying that even though the little triangle is folded onto the rectangle that it's still extra. Does that mean the triangle is bigger?

Harrison: Yep! (Mackenzie also nods in agreement.)

Edith: But if you flip the rectangle over, you'll see a triangle missing on the other side (see Figure 3.16). That little extra triangle matches right there, so it's perfect.

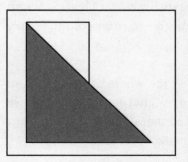

Figure 3.16 Rectangle flipped over

Teacher: What do you mean by, "It's perfect"?

Edith: You can turn the triangle into the rectangle. Can I show how we did it?

Teacher: We'd love to see it.

Edith: We lined up the rectangle and triangle like they did, but we cut the extra piece off of the triangle (see Figure 3.17). Then we moved the extra piece to the top and it made the rectangle. So they're the same (see Figure 3.18).

Harrison: Oh yeah. We didn't see that side.

Teacher: Do you think they are equal now?

Harrison: Uh-huh. They match, so they're the same.

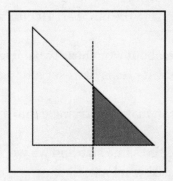

Figure 3.17 Edith's demonstration of where to cut the triangle

Figure 3.18 Edith's construction of another rectangle

Teacher: What did other people do? I'm curious about the people who measured or used tiles.

Davis: We tried measuring with the rulers, but it didn't help us.

Teacher: Can you explain what you tried?

Davis: We measured the sides and got eight here and here (shows the length of the rectangle and one side of the triangle), but then we got four on the rectangle, but there wasn't a four on the triangle and we messed up.

Teacher: What did you do next?

Davis: We cut out the pieces like Edith's group.

Teacher: What about the group with the tiles?

Tatiana: We tried doing what we did when we were measuring rectangles and found out which ones had the most tiles. We left it on the table because we couldn't carry it over here without dropping the tiles.

Teacher: What did you discover?

Tatiana: Well, the rectangle took thirty-two tiles to cover the whole thing. But when we tried to cover the triangle, we could get only twenty-eight tiles to cover. But we saw there were half-tile spaces left over, so we counted them. And if you could cut tiles in half, you could put four more tiles in those spaces.

Hector: So that's thirty-two on both. They're the same.

Mackenzie: I don't know where the four extra tiles come from. Shouldn't it be eight? There are eight spaces left over.

Hector: Those are only half spaces. See? (Points to one half.) If you broke a tile in half, you could put one half here and one half in this other space.

Mackenzie: Oh, I see. So it's 1, 1, 2, 2, 3, 3, 4, 4 (pointing to the numbers Hector wrote in the empty spaces).

Teacher: It seems like we have a lot of ways to think about why these two halves are equal. When we started, it wasn't so clear, but now it seems like everyone agrees. What changed?

Harrison: We showed it a bunch of ways. Like we can make the triangle into a rectangle and stuff like that.

Jeslyn: Well, it makes sense. The sandwiches were the same size and we were just making different halves. A half is a half no matter what it looks like.

Teacher: Interesting. "A half is a half no matter what it looks like." Who agrees with that statement? (A number of hands go up. I want to stay with this idea, but we are running out of time.) I think I'd like us to test that statement tomorrow for math class. We'll see if we can prove that it's true.

In this final vignette, students are working on a mathematical task that's fairly open-ended. There was only one answer, but students could approach it in a number of ways. That's what makes the task so great for MP3. Whenever students have opportunities to approach tasks in their own way, there is room for mathematical arguments and open debate. These students were engaged in productive mathematical discourse because they all had different ideas about why the halves were either equal or not equal.

As with the other vignettes, the teacher keeps the ownership of ideas with the students and merely acts as a facilitator to help keep the discussion going and bring in a variety of ideas. At first the arguments focused on whether one half was bigger and students worked to convince others of their positions. Once it was established that the halves were equivalent, the arguments moved to strengthen the collective agreement of the class. Ms. Perch worked to pull the thinking of students together so that, in the end, students were able to work toward making a conjecture that a "half is a half no matter what it looks like." Her class is now in a position to explore incongruent halves and test the conjecture that halves of the same whole are equivalent even if they don't look alike.

Regardless of how you decide to implement MP3 in your classroom, constructing viable arguments and critiquing the reasoning of others are essential elements in math class. When students have to justify their reasoning, they learn to be mindful mathematicians and that the choices they make should be intentional. The debates that occur during this kind of productive mathematical discourse serve to strengthen students' collective understanding. They learn to rely on each other rather than the authority of the teacher to prove whether a claim is true. The students in Ms. Perch's class provide an excellent example of this kind of interaction.

When we hold the authority as teachers, we often let the students off the hook in terms of their responsibility for articulating, defending, and revising their mathematical arguments. Imagine if Ms. Perch just had students tell her their reasoning and she let them know if their answers were right or wrong. Teachers are a much easier audience for students, because we are listening with the goal of understanding their ideas. We can infer a lot of what students are trying to say, which can make their job much easier because they don't have to work as hard to convince us. However, when we require them to justify their thinking to their peers, it raises the stakes because they have to be much more articulate when stating their arguments.

Also, if we are the only ones a student has to convince, then their classmates are off the hook in terms of having to be active listeners during these math discussions, because they aren't required to make sense of their peers' mathematical thinking. However, when we create a culture where students have to listen to one another and question or critique the reasoning of others, everyone shares the responsibility. One of the best things we can do for our students is give up some of our authority in math class. That's what happened in Ms. Morrissey's room, which allowed for that great exchange between Tariq, Trina, and Autumn about triangles.

Additionally, by providing tasks that allow for multiple entry points and then expecting students to justify their reasoning behind their approaches, students are encouraged to explain and defend their reasoning. The responsibility to prove and disprove ideas falls on the students. To ensure students have ample opportunities to construct viable arguments and critique the reasoning of others, teachers need to create classroom cultures where these types of discussions are the norm. There are clear expectations that creating, defending, and critiquing arguments are a natural part of math class. Each of the teachers in these vignettes worked hard to create that kind of culture in their classrooms, and the kinds of discussions that result from that work help us see how powerful this approach can be.

Over time students will develop more vocabulary and understandings of complex mathematical ideas. As this happens, their arguments and critiques will grow more sophisticated. They will use referents more effectively and eventually move to more abstract ways to describe their reasoning to others. Through constructing and defending arguments as well as carefully listening to or reading the arguments of others, students will strengthen their conceptual understanding of major mathematical ideas.

CHAPTER 4

Mathematical Practice 4: Model with Mathematics

Much to their delight, my wife and I recently introduced the concept of allowances to our children. Before this time, we had routine chores that everyone helped with and chalked up to family work. Now that the kids are a little older and can do more around the house, it made sense to start giving them weekly allowances. We did some research on what's appropriate, modified some ideas, and settled on a rate of fifty cents times the age of each child per week. The idea is that allowances should be a modest amount that the kids have full control over to encourage them to learn how to use and save money wisely. Also, we have differentiated pay because older children can do more and therefore should earn more. For example, my eleven-year-old daughter makes $5.50 per week while my eight-year-old son makes $4.00.

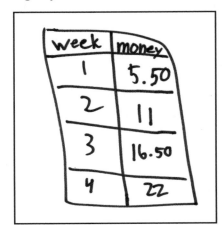

Figure 4.1 Allowance table

When we introduced these rates to the kids, there was some initial groaning from the older ones, who said it wasn't a lot of money. We talked about savings and how they could calculate the amount of money they'd save after a given number of weeks. They created rough tables that looked like Figure 4.1.

What they discovered was that the small amount for one week of work quickly accumulated into a good amount of spending money over time. In fact, once they had the table created, they began talking about what

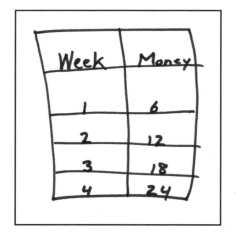

Figure 4.2 Dan's weekly allowance table

they wanted to spend their money on and then calculating how long they'd have to save before they could get it. My two oldest boys wanted a $100.00 Lego set and began working together to plan how they could combine their money and get it faster. My oldest, Dan, said it would take just over four months for him to save up by himself. He then made two tables: one per week (Figure 4.2) and one per month (Figure 4.3).

My nine-year-old, Sean, did the same for his allowance (Figure 4.4).

They then combined their totals in yet another table (Figure 4.5).

When they saw that at three months they would be at $126.00, they went back to two months to see how much more they needed to get from $84.00 to $100.00. They then looked at their weekly rate and saw that after two more weeks they'd have enough. They planned to save for three months and two weeks to buy a $100.00 Lego set and were pretty excited. I didn't spoil their excitement by pointing out that with a 6.25 percent sales tax in Massachusetts, they'd be $1.00 short. We'd address the tax thing before they actually got to the store to buy it, and I figured I'd pony up the extra buck.

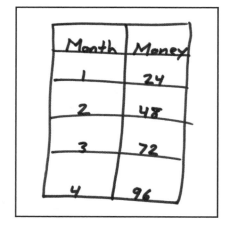

Figure 4.3 Dan's monthly allowance table

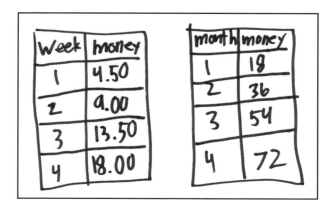

Figure 4.4 Sean's allowance tables

I'm glad my kids had this discussion about savings and allowances—not just because I believe it's important to instill strong money management in my kids, but also because they experienced a great real-life example of modeling with mathematics. They took a contextualized situation of earning and saving an allowance and created a mathematical model using a table to determine how long they would have to collectively save to purchase a Lego set. Although they were focused on finding how long it would take them to get a particular item, their model can be extended to any total amount.

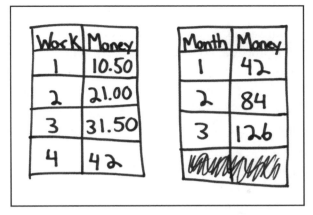

Figure 4.5 Dan and Sean's allowance tables

In full disclosure, I misinterpreted what it means to model with mathematics when I first read the Standards for Mathematical Practice, mainly because of one word: *model.* And that's because we have many meanings for the word *model* in education. Think about the different ways we use that word in the classroom:

Model (verb) — To show how to do something.
The teacher modeled how he wanted students to complete the assignment.

Model (noun) — A small copy of something.
Tasha created a model of her school using Legos.

Model (adjective) — Remarkable, commendable, worthy of being copied.
Juan was a model student during our math discussion.

As common as these uses of the word *model* are in the primary classrooms, none of them have the connotation associated with MP4. One other similar phrase and concept that adds to the confusion is "modeling mathematics," which is different from "model with mathematics." The former refers to using representations to make sense of mathematical ideas. For example, to solve 24 + 32, a second grader might use base ten blocks to show 2 tens and 4 ones being added to 3 tens and 2 ones. In this case, the mathematics is being "modeled" with a physical representation.

To model *with* mathematics means to take a contextualized situation and abstract the math from it to get a better understanding of the situation. In other words, when students model with mathematics, they mathematize the world around them.

This happens all the time in the real world where people abstract contextual situations to analyze what is happening. A city official monitors traffic patterns over time and creates mathematical models to help her understand traffic flow. She might look at the graph she created showing traffic patterns and notice that after 6:00 p.m., the amount of traffic from a particular direction at an intersection drops off. The model informs her decision to adjust the program in the traffic light to run on sensors after 6:00 p.m. A marine biologist uses mathematical models to monitor population densities of great white sharks. Knowing that some sharks travel in pairs and others alone, he is able to use the data from actual shark sightings to predict the total population in a given section of the ocean. Political pundits use mathematical models to monitor the opinions of voters in different geographic areas, allowing them to predict which candidate is most likely to win in particular precincts.

For older students to create, analyze, and make sense of complex models such as the ones listed above, they need a strong foundation that begins in the primary grades and is refined as they get older. K–2 teachers provide the entry point into this work and introduce students to the idea that we can mathematize the world around us.

Let's begin by looking at some basic examples of modeling with mathematics

Figure 4.6 Eliza

to get a sense of what this looks like with young students. The first example (see Figures 4.6–4.10) is from a first-grade classroom where students were working on making lots of different representations of who sits at their tables. Following are some of the responses from five students sitting at the same table (two boys and three girls). Some are examples of modeling with mathematics and some are not.

Each of the students' examples is a correct representation of the members of their table; however, only a few examples abstracted or mathematized the situation. Maverick, Rosie, and Eliza's representations show the context of their group. Eliza drew a picture of the group members, and Rosie listed their names and separated them into boy and girl categories. Maverick did highlight that there are two boys and

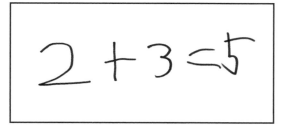

Figure 4.7 Collin

Figure 4.8 Laura

three girls but in the form of a statement rather than an abstraction. These three representations are not examples of students modeling with mathematics, because we can still see elements of the original context.

Collin's example may be easier to identify as a mathematical model than Laura's because he represented the table members in an equation—2 + 3 = 5—representing the two boys, three girls, and five total students at the table. He essentially took a contextualized situation and mathematized it by expressing it in the form of an equation. He could also have represented it with the expression 2 + 3, leaving out the total number of students. In a mathematical model, it is not important that the number *2* represents boys and the number *3* represents girls. What is important is that there are two of one kind of variable and three of another.

Laura's example is a little trickier. She didn't use numbers in her representation but instead used cubes to represent the boys and girls at the table. What makes Laura's representation different from Eliza's is that Laura abstracted the situation, whereas Eliza drew the actual situation in terms of boys and girls. Eliza's drawing is a literal interpretation of the situation; Laura's is an abstraction of the situation. In other words, if you look at Eliza's picture, you could infer the context to which she refers, but you can't infer that with Laura's cube representation. Similar to Collin's equation, Laura's cubes

Figure 4.9 Maverick

have mathematized the situation. She highlighted the mathematical elements of the contextual situation of her table group.

Much of the work in the primary grades around modeling with mathematics focuses on students' abilities to identify and represent the math in contextualized situations. In other

Figure 4.10 Rosie

words, students learn to mathematize situations that are not mathematical in nature. The more opportunities we give students to abstract the math from everyday events, the more practice we give them in modeling with mathematics. For kindergartners, this work begins with more obvious mathematical contexts. It's easier for them to see the math when it's explicit. These experiences help them develop a mathematical mindedness that is necessary for this practice standard.

Let's look at the following example from a kindergarten class that was working on classroom inventories.

|| Focus Questions

1. In what ways does the task below support students in modeling with mathematics?
2. How does Ms. Stevenson push students toward abstraction rather than literal representations?
3. Which students are modeling with mathematics? What evidence supports this assertion?

Can We Show Bears Without Showing Bears?

Ms. Stevenson—Kindergarten, January

My kindergartners can be very literal in mathematics, and understandably so. If I give them a problem such as *There are two blue fish and four red fish in the tank. How many fish are in the tank?* most of my students will draw two blue fish and four red fish, count them, and then say six fish. There is nothing wrong with this approach. Students can successfully solve the problem and represent their thinking using this method. The issue is that drawing fish takes a lot of time and sometimes students get lost in the story and lose the math as they draw.

I set up a math center called *Classroom Inventories* in my room that had various objects in bins on shelves. I also prepared a recording sheet for students as they worked on their inventories (Figure 4.11). They had jobs to do for their inventories. The first was to count the number of objects in each bin and represent that count on their recording sheet. The second job was to identify the bin with the most objects and the bin with the fewest objects.

```
┌─────────────────────────────────────────────────────────────┐
│  Inventory Recording Sheet                                    │
│                                                               │
│  ───────────────────────────────────────────────────────     │
│                                                               │
│                                                               │
│  Bin P:                                                       │
│                                                               │
│                                                               │
│                                                               │
│                                                               │
│  ───────────────────────────────────────────────────────     │
│                                                               │
│                                                               │
│  Bin: Q:                                                      │
│                                                               │
│  ───────────────────────────────────────────────────────     │
│                                                               │
│                                                               │
│  Bin: R:                                                      │
│                                                               │
│                                                               │
└─────────────────────────────────────────────────────────────┘
```

Figure 4.11 Inventory Recording Sheet

I prepared a bin labeled *Bin P* for practice. Inside were nine counting bears from our math manipulatives. I tried picking objects that were hard to draw so students would be less likely to draw the actual objects. I also created a duplicate of the recording sheet on chart paper so the students could see what it looked like. The following is what transpired during this introduction:

Teacher: The first thing we need to do is pick a bin. I think we should go with Bin P for practice. Can I have a volunteer get the bin and take out the objects so we can all see them?

Jocelyn: (Takes the bin down.) Ooh, bears. (Begins placing them on the table so everyone can see.)

Teacher: Great. What do you think we need to do next?

Chen: Count them, like (begins pointing at the bears) 1, 2, 3, 4, 5, 6, 7, 8, 9. There's 9.

Teacher: Thanks for helping, Chen. We talked about how we should check our counting to make sure our counting was correct. Can I have another volunteer come up and check Chen's counting? Sukriti?

Sukriti: (Carefully places one bear at a time from one side of the table to the other as she counts.) One, 2, 3, 4, 5, 6, 7, 8, 9. Nine. Yep, he's right (giggles).

Teacher: Do we feel pretty good that there are 9 bears? (All students nod.) Now what do we have to do?

Andrea: Write it down?

Teacher: Very good. Yes, we have to record our thinking on our sheet. Now, remember we have been talking about how we can record our counting. How can you record?

Andrea: You can put a 9.

Teacher: (Writes *9* on the chart next to Bin P.) Oh, I forgot. Before I record, I have to make sure I'm recording in the right place. What bin are we on?

Students: P.

Teacher: Okay, am I recording in the right place? How do I know?

Chen: It says Bin P on the chart. It matches. See? P-P. (A bunch of giggles erupt. I should have picked a different letter for our practice bin.)

Teacher: Ha ha. Very funny. Yes, we matched the right place to record. Now, who said that we could just write a 9? (Andrea raises her hand.) Yes, that's right. One way we can show how many objects there are is to write the number. Can you come up and write a 9 on our chart? For this activity, you will need to show your thinking two ways. One way is to write the number. How else might we record how many bears are in the bin?

Carmen: Write it?

Teacher: Do you mean with words?

Carmen: Uh-huh. Like write. (She comes up, takes a pen, and writes *nin* on the chart.)

Teacher: Thanks. How else can we show how many are in the bin?

Students: (Silence and shrugs.)

Teacher: Can we draw pictures? (Heads nod.) What might that look like?

Efren: (Comes up and grabs a pen.) I draw them like this. (Begins drawing bears on the chart as shown in Figure 4.12.)

Figure 4.12 Efren's drawing

This was perfect, because he was drawing very detailed bears and taking a long time. I wanted to use the opportunity to highlight this with the students.

Teacher: Wonderful drawings, Efren. I'm going to stop you for a moment. Girls and boys, do you notice how carefully Efren is drawing and how he is putting all of these great details into his picture? This is what we call an artistic drawing. Artistic drawings take a long time to create. In math, we actually use a different kind of drawing called math drawings. What do you think math drawings look like?

Marie: They have numbers.

Teacher: They might, but how do you think a math picture is different from an artistic one?

Marie: Oh, like . . . I . . . Can I come up? (She takes a different-color pen and puts numbers on Efren's picture as shown in Figure 4.13.)

Teacher: You put numbers on the picture. That certainly helps us see the math—very helpful. I guess what I'm wondering is, Efren's drawings are beautiful, but they take a long time to make. I'm wondering if there is a way we can draw a picture to show how many bears are in the bin without drawing bears.

Figure 4.13 Marie's addition to Efren's drawing

Nolan: Like can we show the bears without showing the bears? Like with circles?

Teacher: Sure. What would that look like? (Nolan grabs a pen and draws Figure 4.14.)

Teacher: One way we can show it is to

Figure 4.14 Nolan's drawing

Figure 4.15 Victor

draw very detailed bears, but that might take a long time. Nolan drew circles, which went much faster, but how does Nolan's drawing show us how many are in the bin?

Sukriti: (Comes to the chart.) It goes 1, 2, 3, 4, 5, 6, 7, 8, 9. (She points to each circle as she counts.)

Teacher: And that shows the total number of bears?

Sukriti: Mm-hmm.

Teacher: How do you know?

Sukriti: It goes 1 (points to a circle), 1 (picks up a bear), 2 (points to a circle), 2 (picks up a bear, and so on).

Sukriti did a great job demonstrating how the circles matched the bears in Bin P. At this point, I thought we had been sitting too long and the students understood the activity. We moved on with our day. Over the course of the week students visited the center in small groups and worked in pairs to complete the activity. The student work in Figures 4.15–4.18 shows the range in thinking about the task for Bin A (twelve plastic dogs). As I said, I really wanted students to practice creating abstract representations of the inventory bin contexts. I thought this activity would help them practice that skill. Some approached it more abstractly than others. We'll need to keep practicing, but I'm pretty happy with this first round.

Figure 4.16 Nolan

Figure 4.17 Marie

Figure 4.18 Sukriti

In this task, students were pushed to move past their literal drawings of situations and begin to abstract them with other methods. This is the emerging stage of modeling with mathematics, and it's an important one. Mathematizing contextual situations does not come naturally for young children, and this activity provides a great example of how this early work develops. Helping students learn to create abstract representations is an important step in the right direction.

The task itself had quantities the students had to count and represent, so abstracting it was not too complicated for most of them. As older students work on MP4, they can pull the math out of less mathematical contexts (such as creating a graph of the data collected from school lunch choices). However, young students need contexts where the math is more explicit. Understanding that a circle can represent a plastic dog in a bin is fairly complicated for many kindergartners, so tasks like these are critical in helping students shift to more mathematical representations.

Ms. Stevenson supported students in this task by making the nature of their drawings explicit. By highlighting the fact that there is a difference between artistic drawings and mathematical ones, she is helping them pay attention to how they are representing their mathematical thinking. By encouraging them to use faster methods of drawing, she is also stressing the importance of this kind of work without directly telling them, "I want you to use circles to show your pictures." There is still an element of choice here. Ms. Stevenson is raising the idea that students should be working toward efficient representations, but she is not directing them to one kind of representation. This allows students to approach the task in ways that make sense to them.

Bin A contained twelve objects. As we consider the student work, we see a variety of ways in which students represented that quantity. All but Marie represented the twelve in a way that was removed from the context. Nolan completely mathematized the context by writing *12*. Victor and Sukriti did pictorial representations but abstracted the original context using simple pictures. They demonstrate an understanding of the twelveness of the objects in Bin A without having to draw a literal representation of the plastic dogs like Marie did. There is a subtle difference between the work of Victor and Sukriti and that of Marie, but an important one in the primary grades. It's an early indicator of students beginning to think abstractly about the math within a context.

As students develop their facility with numbers and operations, their work with MP4 becomes more mathematical in nature. They may represent situations numerically as a way to represent the relationships between all the elements of a contextualized situation. They will also begin to use their models to make predictions and draw conclusions about the values in a given scenario. We can see how these ideas grow as we look at the next vignette from a second-grade class.

Focus Questions

1. What are the elements of this task that highlight the fundamentals of MP4?
2. How does the teacher support the range of learners in the classroom as they work on modeling with mathematics?

You Stand in Front of a Guy Getting Yellow

Ms. Larkin—Grade 2, March

My second graders were working on a patterns-and-functions unit and using a context of Everlasting Gobstoppers from the book we were reading, *Charlie and the Chocolate Factory* by Roald Dahl. The Everlasting Gobstopper machine makes gobstoppers of various colors. On one day, the Oompa-Loompas set the machine to make gobstoppers in the following order: green, blue, yellow, white. On another day it might be set to red, red, blue, green, purple.

Early in the unit, students were asked to draw representations or create cube models for various settings on the candy machine and attach values to them (see Figure 4.19).

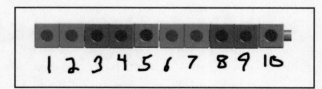

Figure 4.19 Cube model with numbers

Students were asked to consider questions such as *What number is the next blue candy going to be?* and *What color will the sixteenth candy be?* This early work helped students identify the mathematical elements of the candy machine context. As they became more comfortable with this work, I began extending the questions to push their thinking. For example, *What color gobstopper will you get if you are the twenty-fifth person in line? What is the rule for getting green gobstoppers?* These questions were designed to direct students toward mathematical models to find the answers.

It was the last week of our patterns-and-functions unit, and I wanted to push all my students to start using mathematics to solve the candy machine problems. About half the students were doing that, but the other half still built cube models that extended the pattern to answer my questions. I decided to ask questions that would make using a cube model cumbersome in the hopes that most would use a mathematical model.

The candy machine for this set of questions produced candies in a five-element pattern: red, red, green, blue, yellow. (See Figure 4.20.)

The questions I wanted students to work on were as follows:

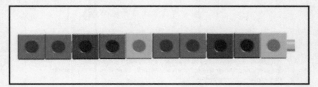

1. What color gobstopper will you get if you are the twenty-fifth person in line?

Figure 4.20 Candy machine pattern for the question set

2. What color gobstopper will you get if you are the fiftieth person in line?
3. If a group of kids wanted to make sure they each got yellow gobstoppers on their trip to Wonka's factory, what would they have to do? Explain your thinking.
4. Bonus: What is the rule for getting a blue gobstopper? A green gobstopper?

I knew not everyone would be ready for the bonus questions, but I wanted to put them out there because I was curious how the group would approach them. Here is the work from a small group I worked with. They had gotten to only the first three questions (Figures 4.21–4.23) when I joined the group, but we talked about the bonus questions and had a good conversation.

Teacher: What did you all discover?

Zak: We didn't get to the bonus yet.

Teacher: That's okay. Tell me about what you discovered.

Zak: The yellows count by fives.

Felicia: Yeah, see? I did a number line to show the fives.

Teacher: So every counting-by-five number is a yellow? How do you know?

Felicia: It's a pattern—you know, 5, 10, 15, 20.

Teacher: But how do you know that pattern will continue?

Name: Vinnie

1. What color gobstopper will you get if you are the 25th person in line?

2. What color gobstopper will you get if you are the 50th person in line?

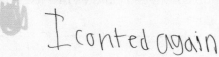

I conted again

3. If a group of kids wanted to make sure they each got a yellow gobstopper on their trip to Wonka's factory, what would they have to do? Explain your thinking.

?

Figure 4.21 Vinnie

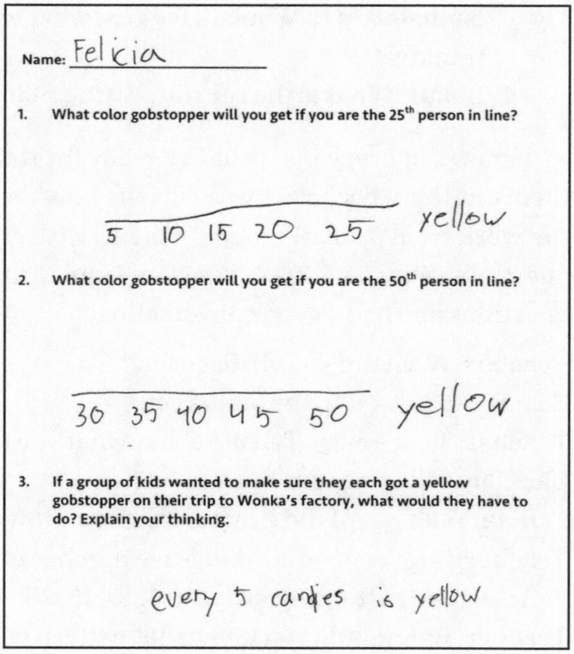

Figure 4.22 Felicia

Name: Felicia

1. What color gobstopper will you get if you are the 25th person in line?

5   10   15   20   25   yellow

2. What color gobstopper will you get if you are the 50th person in line?

30   35   40   45   50   yellow

3. If a group of kids wanted to make sure they each got a yellow gobstopper on their trip to Wonka's factory, what would they have to do? Explain your thinking.

every 5 candies is yellow

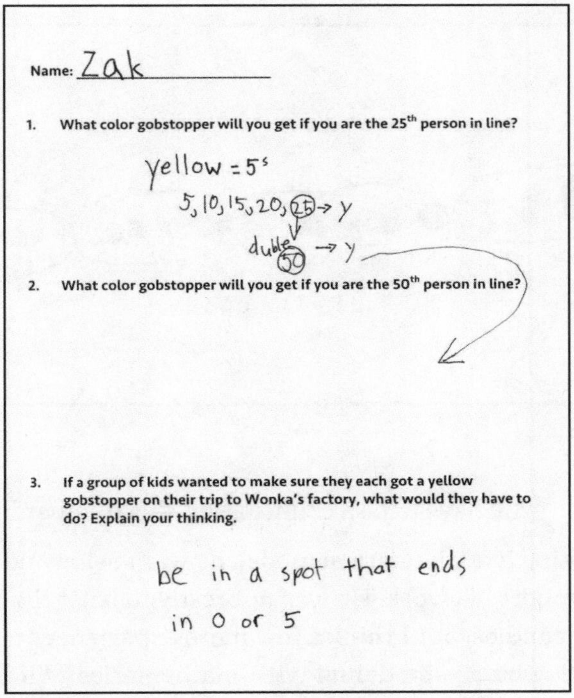

Name: Zak _____

1. What color gobstopper will you get if you are the 25th person in line?

    yellow = 5s

    5, 10, 15, 20, 25 → y

    double 50 → y _____

2. What color gobstopper will you get if you are the 50th person in line?

3. If a group of kids wanted to make sure they each got a yellow gobstopper on their trip to Wonka's factory, what would they have to do? Explain your thinking.

    be in a spot that ends
    in 0 or 5

Figure 4.23 Zak

Zak: It just does. It keeps spitting out candy like this. In fives.

Felicia: And yellow is the last one, so it matches.

Teacher: What do you think, Vinnie? Will yellow always be a counting-by-five number?

Vinnie: (Shrugs.) I guess.

Teacher: What did you discover on your paper?

Vinnie: The pattern goes like (begins circling every five marks on his paper) 5, 10, 15, 20, 25. And then I went (starting at the first circle again) 30, 35, 40, 45, 50. (See Figure 4.24.)

Teacher: Good strategy. Do you see how it connects with Felicia's and Zak's?

Vinnie: Yeah. It's like I made a colorful number line that goes by fives.

Teacher: Vinnie, if I wanted to be sure to get a yellow candy, where would I need to be in line? I notice you have a question mark here, but I'm wondering if our talk has helped you think about this more.

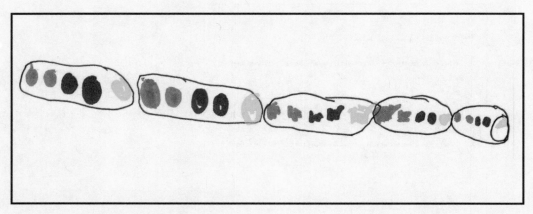

Figure 4.24 Vinnie's paper with circles

Vinnie: Um . . . I think so. . . . It's . . . you have to be a counting-by-five number in line.

Although Vinnie wasn't creating a mathematical model, he was seeing and using the fiveness of the pattern to support his work. He was not ready to trust the mathematics entirely so he drew the candies, but I think a few more experiences helping him connect his work to others who are modeling with mathematics will help. I decided to push on the bonus question to see what they would do with it.

Teacher (to the group): What's the rule then for yellow candies?

Felicia: Every yellow candy is a counting-by-five number.

Teacher: Even big ones, like 456,432,895?

Zak: Well, the machine would probably run out of candy by then, but if it didn't, then, yeah.

Teacher: And how do you know a number is a multiple of 5?

Vinnie: It ends in 5 or 0.

Teacher: You all seem pretty sure about yellow candies. But what if I wanted a blue candy? How would I know where to stand?

Vinnie: Easy—every counting-by-four number. (Felicia nods but looks unsure.) See? Yellow is number 5, but blue is number 4 (pointing to his paper).

Felicia: Yeah, but look (starts pointing to the marks on his picture): 1, 2, 3, 4, 5, 6, 7, 8. Number 8 is green, not blue.

Zak: These all count by fives. They just start different.

Teacher: What do you mean?

Zak: See? (Points to his paper.) Each counting-by-five number has four numbers in front of it like 1, 2, 3, and 4. One and 2 are reds, 3 is green, and 4 is blue.

Vinnie: I don't get it.

Zak: Each of these numbers repeat by fives. Like this first one. Red is number 1. Add 5 to it. What do you get?

Vinnie: Six.

Zak: See? Six is red.

Felicia: Ohhhh. So like 4 and 5 is 9. Nine should be blue.

Vinnie: (Counts on his picture to confirm.) Cool.

Zak: So it's basically right behind a counting-by-five number. Like 4 and 9 and 14.

Vinnie: Like right here (points to his picture shown in Figure 4.25). You just stand behind a guy getting yellow if you want a blue.

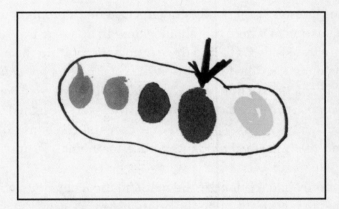

Figure 4.25 Vinnie's picture

Zak: Yeah. Wait, no. You stand in front of a guy getting yellow. It goes red, red, green, blue, and then yellow.

Teacher: The math rule for yellow is that they are multiples of 5. What's the rule for blue?

Felicia: Multiple of 5 take away 1? I think.

Zak: And green is . . . take away 2. Like take 2 away from a fives number. And red is take away 3 and . . . can you say take away 3 or 4?

Teacher: Will taking away 3 or 4 from a multiple of 5 always give you a red?

Zak: (Shrugs.) I'm not sure.

Teacher: I'll leave you three to work some of this out. We're going to come together soon.

I was really impressed with this group's work. Felicia and Zak were using multiplicative models to think about extending the pattern, and their work helped Vinnie make some intuitive leaps in his thinking. Vinnie had a very concrete representation of the candy machine, but he and the others connected it to the mathematical models to confirm their thinking. I intentionally paired Vinnie with Felicia and Zak because I thought he just needed some more experience seeing numerical models for solving problems like these. Zak and Felicia's thinking was just within reach of Vinnie's, so I thought they'd make an excellent team.

The context of a candy machine that spits out candies of different colors in various patterns doesn't jump out at students as a math problem upon first look. However, the question of where one should stand in line to get the candy color he or she desires invites students to find the mathematics within the context and use it to answer the question. The first two—*What color gobstopper will you get if you are the twenty-fifth person in line?* and *What color gobstopper will you get if you are the fiftieth person in line?*—are closed questions that were designed to get students to see some regularity (MP8). The third question and the bonus questions were open-ended and really pushed students to use mathematical models to answer them.

Students not only had to identify the mathematical elements within this context, but also had to pay attention to the relationship between the elements. They needed to see that any multiple of 5 was going to be yellow and that any multiple of 5 minus 1 would result in a blue candy or minus 2 would result in a green. The various mathematical models (number lines, tables, arrays, and so forth) help students make generalizations for answering questions about the context and allow them to see the mathematical relationships among the values.

Additionally, they had to return to the original context after working with their mathematical models to see if their models made sense. Consider the question about where to stand in line for a blue candy. Their rule for the number of candies that are blue was any multiple of 5 minus 1 (for example, 5 – 1, 10–1, 15 – 1, and so on). When asked where you should stand in line to ensure you get a blue candy, Vinnie suggested you should be right behind a person getting a yellow candy. However, Zak considered the model again connected with the pattern (red, red, green, blue, yellow) and pointed out that blue actually comes before yellow. Therefore you would have to be in front of a person getting a yellow to get a blue. The mathematical model helped students solve problems and make generalizations, but with MP4 it is also important to keep checking the original context to make sure the model and assumptions made from the model still work.

Although the task lent itself to MP4, not every student in the class used mathematical models to solve the problem. Vinnie, for example, seemed to understand the pattern and the idea that yellow candies are multiples of 5, but these ideas were still new to him, so he relied on his old standby of physically representing the context. Ms. Larkin supported the range of learners in the room by leaving the task open for students to choose their own solution pathway while purposefully pairing students to support each other.

Ultimately, Ms. Larkin would have liked all her students to model with mathematics for this task. However, not every student in second grade is ready to do that at this point. She kept the problem open to welcome all approaches, because physical representations like Vinnie's allow students to solve the problems but are also easily connected to the mathematical models. Vinnie's picture was helpful as the group used Zak's multiple-of-5 model and Felicia's number line model to work through the bonus questions. Notice how they referred to Vinnie's picture on occasion to demonstrate how their rule for getting a blue or green candy worked. Each member of this group had something significant to contribute, and they all gained a greater understanding of the mathematics as a result of working together.

In essence, modeling with mathematics is a way for students and adults to solve simple and complex problems that they encounter in their lives. The process typically begins with identifying the key mathematical elements of a context, problem, or task. In early grades the mathematical ideas are usually fairly explicit, as we've seen in these vignettes, because the idea that real-life situations can be represented mathematically is new and fairly complex. Young students need lots of opportunities to mathematize contextual situations so they can practice representing. This work can be as basic as asking students to write an equation to match a story situation or as complex as using tables to represent the multiplicative nature of getting a weekly allowance.

Once the mathematical elements have been identified, students can then analyze the relationships between the quantities, shapes, patterns, and so on and draw conclusions based on their observations. Pulling the math out of the context allows students to simplify situations.

Sometimes this work is precise, with students concentrating on finding exact answers like in the *Everlasting Gobstopper* problems. Other times the work is more approximate. For example, when going on a shapes scavenger hunt in the classroom to find circular shapes, kindergartners identified the following objects as circular: the classroom clock, a hexagon pattern block, a circle on the shape board, the stop sign by the door, and their heads. Although we may not consider all of those objects circular, there is a general roundness about them. As the language from MP4 says, "Mathematically proficient students . . . are comfortable making assumptions and approximations . . . realizing these may need revision later." The kindergartners were comfortable approximating the roundness of objects for the scavenger hunt, but will likely revise their list after working with their teacher to further define the term *circular*.

In any case, when students have worked with the mathematical elements, they must also consider the original context and consider whether their solutions and/ or mathematical models make sense. When solutions do not make sense, students must reconsider their models, determine where things went wrong, and possibly revise them for future work. Consider this final exchange from Mr. Sanchez's first-grade class.

|| Focus Questions

1. How does this task support students' work in modeling with mathematics?
2. How does the context of beans and cucumbers help Angelique revise her model?

You Can't Have No Cucumbers

Mr. Sanchez—Grade 1, January

As a way to work on MP4, Model with Mathematics, I began emphasizing how my students could represent situations and problems in other ways besides acting out the actual situations or drawing pictures of the exact context. To support this work, I challenged them with the following task:

I PLANTED 8 SEEDS IN CUPS ON THE SCIENCE TABLE. SOME ARE BEAN SEEDS AND SOME ARE CUCUMBER SEEDS. WHAT COMBINATIONS OF PLANTS CAN WE HAVE GROWING AT THE SCIENCE TABLE? CAN YOU FIND ALL THE COMBINATIONS?

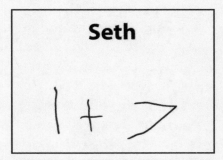

Figure 4.26 Seth

There was a range of responses from my students. Most could find at least one combination that worked for the context as seen in some of the examples shown in Figures 4.26–4.28.

Each of these student work samples was an example of modeling with mathematics but in varying degrees. Students such as Davionne, who are just beginning to transition from literal re-creations of problems to modeling with mathematics, drew pictures but then connected the mathematical elements to the drawings. Students such as Seth wrote one or more equations to demonstrate various combinations. Rubin's example went a step further by showing how you could start with one cucumber and seven bean plants and then remove a value from the bean column and add it to the cucumber column. He did this move only once, so we don't know if he was thinking of extending the model further.

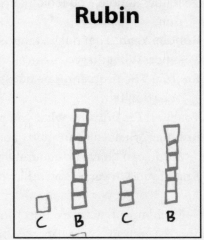

Figure 4.27 Rubin

Figure 4.28 Davionne

However, Angelique did do this as seen in her work in Figure 4.29.

Angelique: This is what I did. I knew there were 8, so I did 0 and 8 'cause that's 8. Then I just did the pattern like this. So I got all the ways.

Teacher: How many combinations of plants can we have?

Angelique: (Counts them.) Nine.

Teacher: And how do you know this works?

Angelique: You just start with 0 plus the biggest number and then go from there. Like if you had 7, you do 0 and 7. Or if you had 6 plants you'd do 0 and 6 and then 1 and 5.

Most kids seemed impressed with her work and did not question it. That's typical with Angelique. She's a very strong math student, so her peers tend not to question her reasoning. However, Robbie looked concerned about something she had said.

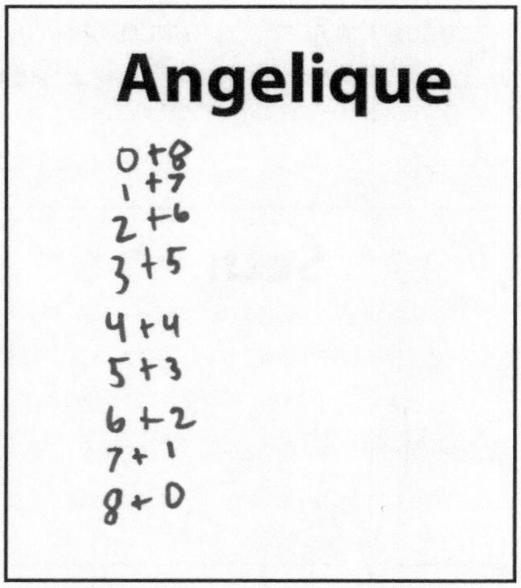

Figure 4.29 Angelique

Teacher: Robbie, you look like you have a question.

Robbie: Yeah. That doesn't match.

Teacher: What do you mean?

Robbie: The problem. The question. You know. It doesn't fit. Well, the first and last ones don't fit.

Teacher: I'm not sure what you mean. Why don't they fit?

Robbie: You need beans and cucumbers. It doesn't say all are beans. If you say 0 plus 8, you can't have no cucumbers. You need both.

Angelique: Oh yeah. So it still works. You just get rid of the zero ones.

Problem structures like these can be categorized as put-together, both-addends-unknown situations. With these structures, we know the sum but do not know either addend. As a result, there are a number of possible answers and approaches to solving the problem. Both-addends-unknown problems allow for students to mathematize contextual situations in an effort to find all possible solutions. Some of these models are visual representations of quantities, and others are strictly numerical.

In this particular example, we also get to see a student who had to revise her model after reflecting on the original context. Angelique created a mathematical model to work through the task and found a very efficient solution pathway. The model was strong, and she even generalized it a bit to work with other total combinations. However, when Robbie's statement caused her to consider the original situation, she realized she had to modify her model to fit the situation. That refinement can then be applied to future problems of a similar nature.

A key component of modeling with mathematics calls for students to reconsider the original context after they have worked with their mathematical models. Going back to the context allows them to consider whether their results make sense or if they need to revise their model further or design an entirely new approach. Students might not return to the original context on their own, so teachers should encourage them to do so as a natural part of the problem-solving process.

Teachers can support this work in ways that draw upon students' personal experiences within their classrooms and throughout their schools. In this way, students begin to see mathematical elements of familiar situations. For example, a teacher asked her students how many steps it took them to get from the meeting area to the cubbies. The results were placed on the line plot, and students used the model to analyze why some get there in fewer steps than others. Walking to the cubbies is a typical routine in most primary classrooms and is not mathematical in nature. However, a question such as how many steps it takes to get there uncovers the mathematical elements of this process for students to explore.

Sometimes these situations are serendipitous, as was the case with a first-grade teacher who had her class mathematize the indoor recess options based on popularity. Rather than tell her class that 6 kids chose to play board games, 3 kids did an art project, and 13 kids played with Legos during indoor recess, she snapped a picture of them playing and later projected it on the screen during the start of her math block. Her students had to pull out the math from the scenario by assigning numbers to each activity based on how many students were doing each activity in the picture and listing the activities in order of popularity that day. They then had to consider how their resulting lists matched the picture that was displayed. This work wasn't part of her plan for math that day, but she noticed something mathematical about the situation and decided to capture it.

More often, this work is carefully planned, based on structures and routines with which students are familiar or from ones provided by the math program a teacher uses. For example, with the Investigations curriculum, second graders collect data on the number of pockets their class has on any given day and create charts to help them determine which day of the week students tend to have the greatest number or smallest number of pockets. When my own second graders did this, they looked at days with the fewest pockets and noticed they fell on days when we had physical education (PE). They concluded that this happened because clothing that students wear on PE days tends to have very few pockets.

Modeling with mathematics is an important skill for students to develop and refine as they engage in authentic problem solving. This work begins slowly in the primary grades as we work to help students see they can mathematize real-life situations. We can foster this kind of thinking by asking questions that drive students to think mathematically about situations and contexts. By drawing students' attention to mathematical elements around them, we help them develop an eye for this kind of work.

As students become more mathematically minded about situations they encounter both in and out of school, they will strengthen their use of mathematical models. We can help this process develop by considering the different contexts and experiences of an average school day that have underlying mathematics not necessarily obvious to students, and work with them to extract the mathematical elements. In the first example of this chapter, my own children used tables to help them plan how long it would take them to save their allowances for a particular Lego set they wanted. My oldest son had lots of experience with tables in his math classes, so it seemed natural to him to use them for this purpose.

Authentic contexts, such as the ones mentioned throughout this chapter, are easily accessible to students and can serve as the backdrop for this work with mathematical modeling. Another source for contexts supporting modeling is the three-act math tasks I mentioned in Chapter 1. These tasks are available on many teachers' blogs and web pages and can be found by searching the web for "three-act math tasks." These tasks present real-world scenarios that students have to mathematize in order to answer questions raised during Act 1 of the tasks.

As you consider emphasizing MP4 with your students, think about the kinds of situations that are meaningful and accessible to them and present the contexts in such a way that the students are responsible for pulling out the math. Opportunities to do this work are plentiful and help students develop a mathematical lens through which to view the world around them.

MP4 is all about mathematizing our world, and the work can be a lot of fun for students as they engage in the process with rich and meaningful contexts. The work begins slowly, with students creating representations that abstract the original context, and then evolves to become more mathematical. As K–2 students develop their skills and understanding of abstracting situations, they build a strong foundation for modeling with mathematics that they will carry with them throughout their mathematical careers.

CHAPTER 5

Mathematical Practice 5:
Use Appropriate Tools Strategically

My daughter, Alli, was a big fan of the show *Cake Boss*. She loved seeing the creative and sometimes unbelievable cake designs come to life on the show and how the different cake designers, especially Buddy, could work through challenges and crises. The show actually inspired her to pursue a hobby of cake decorating, and she quickly accumulated a wide assortment of cake-decorating tools. I remember one of her first creations, which was a haunted-house cake for a Halloween party we were attending. She asked for my help (big mistake), so we broke out all the tools and ingredients and set to work. We discovered very quickly that cake decorating looks a lot easier on TV than in our kitchen. We had all the appropriate tools, but we lacked real strategies and techniques to use them well. We needed help (see Figure 5.1).

My daughter's birthday was that next month, and I got her a cake-decorating lesson at the *Cake Boss* studio in Hoboken, New Jersey. She and I took the class together and were blown away by the experience. There were only eight of us in the class with two of Buddy's nieces as our instructors. They walked us through the basics of how to mix and press

Figure 5.1 Our Halloween cake

fondant, how to frost and wrap a cake, and how to strategize our design. Then we moved on to actual decorating techniques. For our fall-themed cakes, we learned how to make multicolored maple and oak leaves using presses and special cutters. We learned how to properly handle a piping bag to make flowers and write words. They taught us how to select the proper tool for the specific type of design we wanted to create.

Figure 5.2 Our creations

After a lot of practice we started to get the hang of it. The once-overwhelming array of tools and options soon became manageable, and we even started to have fun using them. Alli and I talked about what kind of cake design we wanted and then strategically planned how to accomplish it. It was amazing to see how fast she could select the right tool and use it to create the image she had in her head. When the lesson was over, we had two great-looking cakes to take home with us and the knowledge and skills to use our own tools to make more like them (Figure 5.2).

In our mathematics classrooms, we have a similar scenario. Students have access to a wide assortment of tools that they must learn to use for their mathematical work. The sheer volume of possibilities can seem overwhelming, but with time and experience, students can learn how to choose the right tool for the task at hand and how to use it strategically to reach their goal.

For this to happen, we need to have a solid understanding of the kinds of tools available, the purpose of each tool, and how students can learn to use them flexibly and strategically in any given situation. This also means that we have to make these tools readily available to students, encourage their use, and provide them with options so they can decide which tool to use and how to use it. If we make all the decisions for them, we remove that critical component of MP5 where students make decisions based on their knowledge and understanding of the tools and the task at hand.

MP5 puts forth the idea that tools are a natural part of any K–12 classroom and aren't used just with students who are struggling in mathematics. All students benefit from using tools and learning how to use them for a variety of purposes.

If we don't make tools readily available and value their use, our students miss out on major learning opportunities. Additionally, if we use them only to help students who are having difficulty, we communicate that you need tools only when you struggle. In doing so, we may inadvertently create a stigma around the use of tools whereby students choose not to use them (even if they need them) for fear of looking like they aren't as smart as their peers.

MP5 also brings to light that tools aren't used just for problem solving. Although many math sessions encompass problem-solving elements, there are lots of other ways in which students engage in mathematical thinking where using tools strategically is quite useful. For example, second graders can use manipulatives such as connecting cubes to make representations that highlight the part-part-whole relationship in addition and subtraction to deepen their understandings of the operations. A kindergartner may use pattern blocks to explore how new shapes can be made by combining smaller shapes.

As we explore the components of MP5, let's consider the kinds of tools primary students use before we look at how they learn to use them strategically. In the broadest sense within the context of this practice standard, a tool is anything that helps students with a task. This includes not only standard mathematical tools such as rulers and graph paper, but unconventional tools as well. If a kindergartner uses her classmates' shoes to measure the length of a table, the shoes are tools that help her accomplish the task. For the purposes of this book, we will focus on more conventional tools, but the ideas presented in this chapter can easily be applied to nontraditional tools as well.

According to the Elementary Elaborations of the Standards for Mathematical Practice from the Illustrative Mathematics website (illustrativemathematics.org), tools can be clustered together based on common characteristics. I have taken it a step further by formalizing these clusters into five distinct categories of tools: supplies, manipulatives, representational tools, digital tools, and mathematical tools. The lists below provide examples of specific tools used in primary grades for each category, but the lists are not exhaustive. As you read through them, think about other specific tools you use in your classroom that might fit into each category.

Supplies

These tools are what we typically think of when we consider school supplies. They are the materials students use to do things such as record, create, draw, and measure as they work on math tasks. Supplies are often used in conjunction with tools in the other categories. For example, second graders use 1-inch graph paper and colored pencils along with manipulatives such as 1-inch color tiles to create rectangles of various sizes. Below are some examples of supplies:

- Paper—blank, lined, grid, tracing, chart, construction, paper strips, and so on
- Writing utensils—pencils, pens, markers, colored pencils, chalk, crayons, dry erase markers
- Writing surfaces—whiteboards, chalkboards
- Scissors
- Tape
- Measuring tools—rulers, yard/meter sticks, tape measures, string
- Sticky notes
- Index cards

Manipulatives

Manipulatives include all the tangible, physical objects we often associate with primary mathematics classrooms. They are used for a variety of purposes, including, but not limited to, counting and/or comparing quantities; composing and decomposing shapes or quantities; building patterns, designs, or other creations; developing understandings of shapes, numbers, patterns, fractions, and the behavior of and relationship between the operations; creating representations; and developing and refining strategies for problem solving.

There are a lot of choices of manipulatives from a variety of companies. There are also subtle differences among manipulatives, such as interlocking cubes, that affect how students use them and the options available to them. For example, Unifix cubes connect in only one direction, whereas Multilink cubes can connect on each one of their sides. This distinction might come into play when a student wants to create a rectangular prism using cubes. In this case, the Unifix cubes are much harder to use because each row of cubes cannot connect to other rows, so the figure falls apart easily. That student may find that Multilink cubes are a better option for creating the structure.

The following are some common examples of manipulatives found in primary and elementary classrooms:

- Interlocking Cubes
  - Unifix cubes
  - Multilink cubes
  - Snap cubes

- Blocks
  - Pattern blocks
  - Geoblocks
  - Base ten blocks
  - Attribute blocks
  - Cuisenaire rods
  - Tangrams
  - Color tiles
- Geoboards
- Counters
  - Chips
  - Bears
  - Two-color counters
  - Colored chain links

Representational Tools

Representations serve a variety of purposes. They help students see structure within our number system (MP7), which contributes to the development of number sense. They can be used to solve addition and subtraction problems. They also allow students to represent mathematical ideas or express their reasoning. Representations are unique in that they can be made (or bought) and set out for students to use when they need them or created in the moment by students or teachers. The following are examples of representational tools:

- Number charts (hundreds, fifty, and so on)
- Number lines
- Ten frames
- Number racks
- Tally marks
- Line plots
- Tens and ones strips

Digital Tools

Digital tools involve the use of technology to help students complete math tasks. Some digital tools simply replicate physical or representational tools (such as virtual manipulatives or number lines on an interactive whiteboard). Other digital tools such as calculators or apps that allow students to show their work using multimedia features serve specific purposes based on their capabilities.

We must decide which digital tools we want students to access and for what purpose. The technology can be exciting for students to use, and they may gravitate toward those options over traditional versions if both are available to them. However, getting out iPads and going through the process of opening an app that provides virtual interlocking cubes may not be as efficient as simply getting some interlocking cubes from the bin.

Other times, digital tools provide elements that other tools cannot. For example, when students want to build designs out of pattern blocks, the virtual manipulatives require them to consider the direction and degrees they need to turn the blocks to make them fit. This makes the rotational work much more explicit than when they just build with the blocks. Ultimately, it's up to us to decide when and if a digital tool is an option we want students to explore for a particular lesson.

Here are some examples of digital tools:

- Calculators
- Tablets
- Interactive whiteboards
- Apps
- Virtual manipulatives
- Digital scales

Mathematical Tools

This category of tools is a bit more abstract, particularly for primary-grade students. The Elementary Elaborations of the Standards for Mathematical Practice talk explicitly about how estimation, strategies, and algorithms are all examples of mathematical tools. At first I had a hard time wrapping my head around the idea of strategies being mathematical tools. I was thinking about tools only as physical objects or representations and not as mental constructs. However, one day I was working with teachers on how we support students' development of multiple strategies for solving addition and subtraction problems. In an effort to make my point I said that students having only one approach to solving a subtraction problem is equivalent to having only a hammer in your toolbox. Sure, if you needed to cut a piece of wood, you could hack through it with the back end of the hammer, but a saw would be much better for the job.

Mathematical tools are generalized mathematical approaches to use when working on a task. They are part of students' mental toolboxes. For example, a first grader might decide to estimate the number of triangle pattern blocks needed to fill a shape to decide how many to get from the bin, whereas her partner decides to get the exact amount, calculating the total by adding 6 + 6 + 6 based on the knowledge that three hexagons covered the shape perfectly and six triangles covered one hexagon. In this case, each student uses a different mathematical tool (one student estimating and one student counting up) to decide how to approach the task.

Unlike other tools that are provided to students, mathematical tools must be developed over time. Students aren't hardwired with estimation skills or the ability to quickly decompose numbers by place value. They need experiences that expose them to these tools and then ample practice using them so they become part of the students' repertoires. Mathematical tools in the primary grades include the following:

- Estimation
- Counting
    - Counting all
    - Counting on or back
    - Counting groups
- Composing and decomposing numbers and quantities
- Place value
- Derived facts
- Numerical reasoning

A lot of tools are available in our classrooms, from common, everyday supplies to specialized math manipulatives such as Geoblocks (a set of rectangular and triangular prisms) to mathematical tools such as estimation. MP5 emphasizes that students should become familiar with the choices they have, learn when certain tools are more appropriate than others, and develop strategic ways to use them. For this to happen, we need to build in lots of opportunities for students to learn about the range of tools and then give them experiences where they have to make choices about what tools to use and how to use them.

A large part of our work with MP5 involves developing and supporting our students' metacognition. A constant reflective process occurs when students work on mathematical tasks or engage in mathematical explorations. First, they must consider whether they actually need a tool. If so, they then need to decide which tool or tools would make the most sense in that particular situation and how they could best use it to achieve their goal. Finally, they must reflect on their results to see if they make sense and if the tool they chose was in fact the best one for the job. If it was, they can work on refining its use. If it wasn't, they must go back and consider what other tools might be more useful. Although the work is not always so straightforward and linear, those are the kinds of considerations students must make when working with tools.

This kind of metacognition is difficult with primary students, who don't have a lot of experience thinking about their own thinking. To support them, we must make the metacognitive process explicit to students. We can do that during our whole-group time with the entire class, with small groups, or with individuals working on their own. By asking students a question such as *What math tool might help you work through this task?* we convey that first, there are multiple options, and second, students have a choice in the process. This puts the ownership of this responsibility on the students. It lets them know that they have to consider what tool might best serve them in their task or exploration.

Math discussions provide a great way to support students in this metacognitive process. They are opportunities for students to talk about their mathematical thinking with their peers, with the teacher acting more as a facilitator guiding the discussion and allowing students to own most of the ideas. Math discussions can be used to share strategies, talk about generalizations, discuss conjectures, ask questions, and so on. The following vignette from a first-grade class highlights how well math discussions support the development of MP5.

Focus Questions

1. How does Ms. Mitchell help her students begin to pay attention to the tools that they're using?
2. How does the math talk routine support this work?
3. What other tasks could you do with your students that would provide a context to make this work with tools explicit?

When We Count, We Need Things, and When We Don't, We Don't

Ms. Mitchell—Grade 1, January

When I wanted to explore using appropriate tools strategically with my first graders, I immediately thought of using math talks as the launching point for this work. I have been using math talks for a while now, and a large part of our work has involved students sharing their strategies and the tools they used to solve problems. However, I never really considered how this work was developing students' facility with MP5 until I was in one of my graduate classes and my professor was talking about the differences between physical, digital, and mathematical tools. As he spoke, I thought about all the math talks I do with my kids and how they help students learn to use both physical and mathematical tools.

What I hadn't done until then was make the use of tools explicit for students. We engaged in math talks as a way to share strategies and talk about our mathematical ideas, but I had never communicated to students that these strategies were a form of mathematical tools. For this math talk, I wanted to work with my first graders to develop a chart of tools to which they could refer in future math work.

I wrote *13 + 7* on a sheet of chart paper and asked students to try to solve it. Lots of students started counting on their fingers, but others looked around the room at our number line or hundreds chart. A few asked if they could get some cubes to work it out. I also have a few students who can solve problems in their head fairly quickly, so I knew they were ready right away, but I wanted to give time for my counters to arrive at their answer. Once most students had their thumbs up (our nonverbal cue that they are ready), I began the talk.

Teacher: Before we begin sharing today, I want to talk to you about tools. Who can tell me what a tool is?

Cathleen: You mean like a screwdriver?

Teacher: That's exactly what I mean. What does a screwdriver help us do?

Kash: Screw stuff together . . . like batteries.

Teacher: Great. So if we have a job to do like put batteries in one of our favorite toys, we can use a screwdriver to help open the place where we put the batteries.

At this point other students started calling out different tools such as hammers, saws, and so on. I didn't want the conversation to focus too much on carpentry tools, so I shifted the discussion back to math.

Teacher: It seems like you know lots of tools we can use to make things or fix things. Did you know that you also use tools to help you do math? (Rosalie starts waving her hand.) Yes, Rosalie?

Rosalie: My dad uses a chain saw.

Teacher: For math?

Rosalie: (Giggles.) No, to cut wood and trees.

Teacher: Well, that is another good example for the tools we talked about earlier. Do you have an example for a tool we use to help us with math?

Rosalie: You mean like when we use cubes?

Teacher: Yes, exactly. Cubes are a great example of a tool we use to help us in math. I see a lot of hands up to share math tools. We're going to talk a lot about math tools during our math talk this morning, so when you share your strategy for 13 plus 7, I'd like you to think about whether you used a tool to help you. Who'd like to go first?

Nick: I didn't use a tool. I just did it in my head.

Teacher: Can you explain what you did?

Nick: I just counted in my head.

Teacher: That sounds like a great strategy. What number did you start counting with?

Nick: Thirteen.

Teacher: Then what did you do?

Nick: I counted 1, 2 . . . I mean, 14, 15, 16, 17, 18, 19, 20.

Teacher: How did you know when to stop counting?

Nick: I counted my fingers. (Holds up seven fingers.)

Teacher: So you used a counting strategy? I'm wondering about what you said about tools, though. You said you didn't use any tools, but I'm thinking you did. Not every tool in math is something you get off the shelf.

Nick: Ohhhh. My fingers! I get it.

Teacher: Yes, your fingers were a tool you used to keep track. But there's another kind of tool in math that I like to call thinking tools. These are the strategies you use. Nick said he counted to get his answer and he started at 13. Does anyone remember what we call that strategy?

Olivia: Count-on!

Teacher: Yes! Nick used a thinking tool of counting-on, and he used his fingers as a tool to keep track. I'm going to write these on this chart here:

TOOLS FOR MATH

Thinking Tools	Physical Tools
Count-On	Fingers

Teacher: Did anyone else count on using their fingers? (A few hands go up.) What did others do?

My goal here was to get students noticing that their specific strategies are considered tools. At some point I'd like to create a visual for them to see these as tools in their mental toolbox, but for now I just wanted get them thinking about their strategies as thinking tools.

Loie: I used the cubes. (Holds up two stacks of cubes.) I went 1, 2, 3, 4, 5, 6, 7, 8, 9, 10, 11, 12, 13 and got 13, and then I went 1, 2, 3, 4, 5, 6, 7 and got 7. Then I went 1, 2, 3, 4, 5, 6, 7, 8, 9, 10, 11, 12, 13, 14, 15, 16, 17, 18, 19, 20. So it's 20.

Teacher: What tools did Loie use?

Ezra: Cubes and her brain (giggles).

Teacher: Yes, she used cubes and she did use a thinking tool. What strategy did she use as her thinking tool?

Chen: She counted.

Teacher: Yeah, she did. Did she count the same way as Nick?

Anastasia: No, she counted cubes and Nick counted his fingers.

Teacher: True, they both counted different things, but I'm wondering if there was something different about the way they counted. We said Nick used the count-on strategy. Did Loie use the count-on strategy? (Some kids shake their heads.)

Mikal: She did count-everything.

Sage: It's count-all.

Teacher: We can say it either way. Count-everything and count-all mean the same thing, right? Let's add that to the chart.

TOOLS FOR MATH

Thinking Tools	Physical Tools
Count-On	Fingers
Count-All (everything)	Cubes

I was glad we spent time earlier in our math talks naming strategies. I feel like it helped make this section run more smoothly. We heard from many more students and added each new idea to our chart. Over time it looked like this:

TOOLS FOR MATH

Thinking Tools	Physical Tools
Count-On	Fingers
Count-All (everything)	Cubes
	Number line
	100 chart
	Tally marks
	Pictures
Facts we know	
Breaking numbers up	

I was impressed with our list. They included the physical tools we typically use, and we didn't try adding things to the list that we haven't used. I was kind of expecting some kids to start making up some tools just to be original. Instead, they focused on what they were using. Kids noticed that we used a lot of counting tools (either counting-on or counting-all). Ezra closed our session by making a really astute observation.

Ezra: It's like when we count, we need things, and when we don't, we don't.

He was referring to the list where we had lots of things students used when they used a counting strategy. He noticed that for the numerical strategies of using a fact we know or decomposing numbers, no physical tools are used. This seemed like a great place to leave the discussion. My plan is to leave the list up so we can refer to it for future math work involving addition or subtraction. I also plan to have us add to the list as we discover and use new tools.

In this vignette Ms. Mitchell made the use of tools explicit for her students by directly raising the topic at the start of their math talk. She began by asking students about their knowledge of tools in general before making an analogous comparison to the tools we use in math class. By starting the conversation this way, Ms. Mitchell was helping her students become cognizant of the fact that there are a variety of tools they can use and that she was interested in hearing about their choices.

When Nick announced that he didn't use a tool because he solved the problem in his head, Ms. Mitchell used that opportunity to raise the idea of mathematical tools. In this case she named them thinking tools because that phrasing seemed more accessible to her students. Before this work they had been naming strategies as a way of discussing how different students approached problems. Ms. Mitchell linked this work to the current conversation by referring to these strategies as tools. This was a great way to help students see that in addition to physical tools available in the classroom, their particular strategies were another form of tools. She also helped them see they have choice in those as well by valuing the different mathematical tools that were shared.

By naming our strategies as tools, we can analyze each of them to determine when one is particularly useful and when it is not. This gets at the crux of this practice standard, which is using appropriate tools strategically. As Ms. Mitchell brings this tool chart into future math conversations, she can ask her students questions such as these:

- When is a counting strategy useful?
- Which number should you hold in your head when using the count-on . strategy?
- What is a more efficient way to draw pictures to count?
- Which strategy has fewer steps?
- Can we count the cubes by groups?
- How can knowing 5 plus 5 help us think about 5 plus 6?

Those are just a few suggestions, but they give you a sense of the kinds of question we can ask students to get them thinking about how to use a particular tool strategically. It doesn't matter if the tool is a physical tool or a mathematical tool. Some students consciously make decisions with regard to using tools, whereas others follow what their peers are doing or use tools that are familiar to them. When choices are brought to the attention of the whole class and discussed, students who already make these decisions can become more mindful of using these tools strategically, and others can learn they have options.

We want to make a habit of involving our students in deciding which tools to use and asking them to talk about their choices and the reasons behind them. Then we want them to reflect on the effectiveness of those choices so they can revise their thinking and become more strategic. Using tools strategically is a habit of mind that develops when students are involved in the process and made aware of the effects their choices have on their solution pathways for a given task or the kind of information that is revealed in a math exploration. For example, a student might notice that his cube representation highlighted the tens and ones relationship of his place-value strategy for addition while his number line representation hid those elements.

Math discussions provide a great way for students to talk about their own thinking, the choices they made, and the questions they still have. In terms of supporting MP5, this format allowed students to discuss what tools they used and how they used them, and to connect their strategies to the ones used by other students. These conversations help topics like these rise to the surface. Also, by allotting math time to discuss these ideas, Ms. Mitchell was communicating to her students that these decisions are important and deserve our attention.

We can imagine future math conversations in which Ms. Mitchell and her students talk about how they can best use a count-on approach and when that strategy might not be as helpful. Or another conversation later in the school year about whether using base ten blocks is a more efficient way to solve a problem using place value than drawing sticks and dots. As a result of these kinds of discussions, students become more mindful about the choices they make regarding the tools they choose and how they use them.

This shift is key. Once students start thinking about how they are using the tools available to them, there is more intention behind their work. They work on tasks more purposefully instead of simply trying to get an answer. They consider which strategy makes the most sense given the set of information they have and refine their approach over time. Problem solving and mathematical explorations require strategic thinking, and MP5 really gets at the heart of this.

The next vignette looks a bit more specifically at how we get students to become more mindful of how to use physical tools strategically. It is from my own classroom when I was working on MP5 with my students. It was early in the year, but I wanted my second graders to think about *how* we use tools and to make this metacognition part of our natural math conversation.

One main idea I want to highlight with this vignette is that we can modify just about any unit, lesson, or task to bring out the elements of MP5, because regardless of how tasks and activities are framed in a book, students will need at least one kind of tool listed at the beginning of this chapter to engage with them. Even if the math program you're using does not emphasize elements of MP5 in their materials, you can add it in by making some minor changes: providing additional materials, allowing students to choose among them, and then having a discussion about how the materials helped or didn't help; giving students one tool but asking them to consider the best way to use it; or allowing students to solve tasks or explore mathematical ideas using strategies that make sense to them rather than requiring them to use only one method.

Focus Questions

1. What are the benefits of making students' strategies and choices a central focus of the discussion?
2. What are the challenges of doing this?
3. Can you think of other classroom routines in your room that you can use to help students think about using tools more strategically?

I'm Not Sure About Just Dumping and Counting

Mr. Flynn—Grade 2, September

In the following vignette from my second-grade class, my students were learning about one of our routines from the Investigations curriculum called *Pocket Day*. For this routine, students had to determine the number of pockets they each had on their clothes and then get one cube for each pocket. Then, as a class, they had to figure out how many pockets the class had in total. This was their first day with the activity, and it seemed like a prime opportunity to explore MP5 because there were a variety of ways they could approach the task.

When I knew I wanted to make MP5 more explicit in this task, I thought about modifying it by not directing students to get a cube for each pocket and instead allowing them to choose how they wanted to keep track of that information. I was thinking that they could try different tools and then we could decide which was best. But when I considered the mathematical goals of the lesson, it felt like having students do all that work in the beginning when they were first learning the routine would be too much. I made a note to explore the idea with them at a later time when we did *Pocket Day* again.

Instead, I decided to focus on having the students work out how to use the cubes strategically. In this case, I gave them the tool and asked that they work out the best way to use it to determine the total number of pockets in the class. I wanted them to come up with a bunch of different strategies and then analyze which were most helpful. At this point in the vignette, each student has determined the number of pockets he or she has, taken the equivalent number of cubes, and joined us on the floor in a large circle.

Teacher: You each found out how many pockets you are wearing today. Now we want to figure out how many pockets we have altogether. How can we do that? (A bunch of hands shoot up.)

Maya: We can count the cubes.

Teacher: Was anyone else thinking of this same strategy? (Most hands go up.) What other things can we do?

Casey: We can add up each of our pockets. Like I have 4 and Justin has . . . (looks at his cubes) 5. So that's 9. We can just keep adding.

Teacher: That's another strategy. Who else was thinking about that approach? (A few hands go up.) Any other ideas? (No hands are raised.)

Teacher: If we were going to count the cubes, how should we do it? Make sure you also tell us why you think that's a good idea.

Graham: Dump them in the middle and count them. Then we'd know which ones we still have to count.

Teacher: And how would you count them? What would you do?

Graham: I'd say 1, 2, 3 (mimics pointing to cubes as he counts).

Teacher: Okay, Graham suggested we dump them in the middle and then count them by ones. Is there another idea of how we can count them?

Joey: I'm not sure about just dumping and counting. They'll get mixed up. What if we just count the ones we have and go around?

Teacher: I'm not sure I understand. Can you say more?

Joey: Well, if I go first and I have 2 pockets. I can say 2. Then Chelsea goes and she has 4, so she would say 4 and then we go around.

Chelsea: I wouldn't say 4. I have 4—

Joey: Oh yeah. I mean she would say 6, because 2 and 4 is 6. Then Kaylee goes and says, 7, 8, 9, 10 'cause she has 4, too.

Teacher: Okay, and did you tell us why you think that's a good approach?

Joey: I don't know. It's just . . . they don't get all mixed up like if we made a big pile.

Teacher: Graham suggests dumping them in the middle and then counting the pile by ones so we can keep track of what's been counted. And Joey is saying that we each take the cubes we have and take turns counting around the circle so we don't get our cubes all mixed up. That's kind of like what Casey suggested earlier, right? Didn't you suggest we add up each of our pockets? (Casey nods.) Any other suggestions?

Jestina: Can we count them by tens?

Teacher: How might we try that?

Jestina: Like if you counted out ten and stuck 'em together. Make a bunch of tens. You know, like stacks? (There are some nods of agreement to this suggestion.) It's easy to count by tens.

Teacher: Okay, so we can put them in a pile and count by ones, hold on to the cubes and go around the circle counting by ones, or make stacks of ten with the cubes and count them by ten. Any other ideas?

Although I thought Jestina's suggestion was probably the most efficient and strategic use of the cubes for this activity, I did not want to stop gathering suggestions if there were still more out there. Earlier in my teaching I used to "fish" for the right answer, and once it was given, I would stop the idea generation. I learned from experience that keeping the conversation open removed my judgment from the discussion and kept the ownership with the students. In this case, it would be up to students to decide which approach was most strategic.

Fiona: We could make stacks of five and count by fives. I like counting by fives better.

Jeremiah: We can put them in twos. Twos are easy.

Maeve: How about stacks of twenty?

Stephen: Eights!

Chris: Twelves!

Teacher: Wow, lots of ideas are flying out. It seems like we could put the cubes in stacks of different amounts and count by that number? (Heads nod.) How are you coming up with the number you want to count by? What's important here?

Fiona: You want something you know. Like I wouldn't say sevens.

Teacher: Okay, Fiona says we should count by a number we can skip-count by. You're saying counting by sevens is not one you know?

Fiona: Yeah. I can do tens and fives and twos and . . . well, ones obviously. But not things like eights or twelves.

Teacher: Of all the ones listed on our chart, which ones make the most sense to count by?

Maeve: Twenties!

Teacher: Why?

Maeve: Because it gets rid of the most cubes. You only need like two stacks or something.

Joey: I don't even know how to count by twenties.

Chris: I say count by twelves.

Teacher: And why do you think that's the best way?

Chris: (Shrugs.) I don't know. It's easy, I guess.

Jestina: Counting by twelves is hard.

Teacher: It seems like some numbers are easy for some, but harder for others. How does counting by twelves feel to you all?

Students: Hard.

Teacher: What about counting by twenty? (There is a mixed response. Most seem to think it is hard, but a few students say that it's just like counting by twos.)

Fiona: I say we do fives or tens because everyone knows how to count by those.

Students: Yeah.

Teacher: So you all agree that using the cubes to count by fives or tens is the best way for us to count right now?

Jestina: We can do both. Count by tens first. Then break the stacks in half and do it by fives after.

Teacher: Oh, kind of like a way to check our counting? (Lots of agreement from the students.) How come nobody is suggesting the counting by ones anymore? Fiona said we should pick numbers we know how to count by. You all know how to count by ones.

Maya: It's faster to count the trains. (That's what she calls stacks of cubes.)

Joey: We should also count by ones just to be sure we did it right.

The class agreed to make stacks of ten and to compare stacks to make sure they were the same height. We then counted the four stacks and three leftovers as a class. We checked our counting using Jestina's idea of breaking the stacks in half and counting by fives. Both times the students correctly counted forty-three cubes. Finally, we had Joey lead us in counting the cubes by ones just to make sure our counting was correct. It was helpful to end on that, because it gave us a chance to compare counting by groups with counting by ones.

Teacher: When we started this task, we had lots of ideas about how we could count the cubes. This happens a lot in math. You choose a tool to help you, but you have to decide how to use that tool. Today our tool was the cubes, and you decided the best way to use it was to count them by tens and then check our counting by fives and ones. One thing we want to get in the habit of doing is thinking about our choices and how those choices worked or didn't work for us. What did you think about our counting choices today?

Fiona: I liked them.

Teacher: Can you say more? What did you like about them?

Fiona: Uh . . . I don't know. I just liked them.

Maeve: I would have counted by twenties because it was faster.

Teacher: Maeve would have preferred a different choice today. What's nice is that a lot of times you'll be doing tasks on your own and you can each make the choice that feels right to you.

Jestina: I think tens worked best because we all know how to do tens.

Teacher: Yeah, that makes sense. You chose a strategy that everyone knew since we were doing this as a group.

I ended this discussion by reminding students to think about the choices they have when counting and to think about those choices in future activities when they have to count. I wrote the counting strategies on a piece of chart paper to display in the room so we could refer to it during upcoming counting tasks. All in all, I think this was a very useful discussion to help us think about using cubes more strategically. It took a little longer than the lesson would have if we hadn't emphasized MP5, but I think these conversations are important and worth the additional time.

The benefit of taking the extra time to discuss their strategies is that it allows the ideas to come from the students and not from me. That means they have opportunities to hear mathematical arguments from their peers and to critique their reasoning (MP3). It also helps create ownership of the ideas and changes the power structure in the classroom by showing that we all contribute to the learning in math class. Additionally, because we leave it open to discussion, a much greater variety of strategies reach the surface, making the activity accessible to everyone. It helped students see that there are a lot of choices and that we need to make decisions on what makes sense for us as we do this work.

At the same time, making decisions adds extra time to our math sessions, which is a challenge. I could have just told the kids that at this point, counting by tens is best, and then just had them count. It would have cut the time in half, but it also would have robbed the students of that powerful discussion and the opportunity to make their own choices and have ownership of the work.

As teachers, we have to weigh these options and make decisions that we think make the most sense at any given time. What is helpful with all the MPs is that investing time in any of them is worthwhile because they embody the behaviors and habits of mind of mathematically proficient students. The MPs span the grades, and students will continually be asked to refine their facility with them. For these reasons, carving out extra time to bring students' attention to them seems like a worthy investment.

At the beginning of this chapter, I said the myriad of choices of tools and how to use them can be overwhelming for students, particularly young ones who are just entering this mathematical world. However, we can reduce that sense by being intentional in the tasks we set, the tools we make available, and the time we devote to having students discuss their reasons for choosing tools and the strategies behind their use of them.

Tasks

The tasks we select for students, whether they involve problem solving, a mathematical game, exploring an idea, or something else can have a significant influence on students' work with MP5. Whether you're using a specific math program or pulling from multiple resources, you can tell if a task supports this standard by considering a few key elements of it. First, does the task allow for various options in terms of tool selection and/or tool use, or does it tell students what to do and how to do it? Some tasks will actually say right in the directions, "To solve these addition problems, use cubes to make stacks of ten and ones, and then add them."

If the task doesn't allow for flexibility and student choice, consider changing the instructions a bit to add those elements when you want to focus on MP5. You can rephrase the above directions to say, "Solve these problems," let students know they have lots of choices in resources, and allow them to make those choices. The task is still the same, but we put the onus of how what to use and how to use it on the students. Another option would be to give the modified version of the directions but begin the session by asking students to brainstorm what the best tools would be and how they could best use them. The second way is a bit more targeted, but the ownership of the thinking still lies with the students.

Not every task has to be open-ended and allow for students to make choices, but when we make all the decisions for the students, we aren't emphasizing the critical elements of MP5. There are some days when our mathematical focus is somewhere else and we want to use a more directed activity. However, when one of our goals for a given day is to emphasize this standard, we want to analyze the tasks and activities to make sure there are options for students and that we make time to discuss them.

Available Tools

If we want our students to have options in terms of tool selection and use, then we must ensure that we make those options available. You can use the categories of the initial lists at the beginning of the chapter to help you consider your own inventory. That way you'll know if you have materials and resources that span each category and which ones you find useful for your classroom. You certainly don't need every manipulative on the market, but it will be good to know if you are missing any key materials that might support your students during math.

It's also very helpful to store the materials in specific places that are easily accessible to students. I used a low set of shelves and a bookcase to keep various plastic bins of manipulatives. These shelves always had interlocking cubes on them, but I would also swap other manipulatives in and out, depending on which unit we were doing. This helped limit the choice of materials but still provided options for students. I also had a supply station set up where students could find lots of the materials such as different kinds of paper and writing tools.

One strategy I found very helpful in terms of managing how students went about getting tools was to talk with them in the beginning of the school year about how we could build a mathematical community where students could move around and gather materials they needed in a safe and productive way. Essentially I worked with them to create a set of guidelines that served as our classroom rules during math class. Because they had ownership of the guidelines, the students often monitored their own behaviors, which significantly limited the number of issues.

Because materials were easily accessible to my students, using tools became a regular part of math class and there wasn't a stigma that tools were for kids who struggled. The tools became a means of sense making in the class. Some students used them to help them solve problems, and others used them to create representations of some of the complex numerical strategies. Had I kept them all in a closet and brought them out only when somebody was stuck or only for certain problems, I would have deprived my students of valuable resources to support their mathematical growth.

Taking Time to Talk Tools

By devoting classroom airtime to the topic of tool selection and use, we convey to our students that these decisions are important and that we value their choices and strategic thinking. Over time, students will internalize our interactions and classroom discussions that ask them to consider the tools they plan to use and how they plan to use them. When this happens, students will truly demonstrate that they can use appropriate tools strategically.

We can engage in this kind of talk in whole-group settings at any point during a math class. If we do it in the beginning of a session, we can help students think about these ideas before they engage in a particular task or activity. If we have the discussion at the end, we provide students an opportunity to reflect on their work with tools and to consider the choices they made. These whole-group discussions allow for students to hear from their peers about the range of tools they used and the different ways in which they used them. Connections can be made between different strategies to broaden students' perspectives, and we can encourage students to construct viable arguments for their decisions (MP3).

We can also engage in these conversations in small groups or with individual students as they are working. As you approach a table where students are working, ask them to describe what they're doing and why they chose a particular manipulative or representation. You can ask them to consider how another manipulative or representation would affect their work. This may prompt them to approach the task a second way with a new set of tools. We can then have a conversation about what they learned from engaging in this work in two different ways.

Making an effort to discuss why students choose certain tools and how they decide to use them is a powerful way to bring MP5 to life in your classroom. It communicates to the students that these ideas are important and that you value their thinking and the decisions they make. It also lets them know that we might have to revise our thinking or try other tools if our first choice didn't produce the kinds of results we hoped for. In essence these discussions provide a narrative to support students in thinking about their intention behind the use of tools in class.

When I first considered this practice standard, it seemed very easy and obvious to me. We use tools constantly in the primary grades, and kids do get more strategic with them over time. However, once I began working specifically on MP5 with students, I realized that the complexity of the metacognition involved when students engage in this work is astonishing.

There is a lot to consider when someone is truly thinking about using tools strategically. Once we map out the thought process involved, we can see the complexity of this standard. This level of metacognition is a lot to expect of five- to eight-year-olds, which is why much of our work as teachers in the primary grades involves engaging in this process with the whole class or small groups. We model this habit of thinking when appropriate within our lessons and ask students about their choices when opportunities arise.

Ultimately, we can draw attention to using appropriate tools strategically during any lesson. Rarely are there moments when tools, whether physical or mathematical, are not appropriate. However, we do not need to make this work explicit in every lesson. As with other standards for mathematical practice, we can decide when to emphasize these ideas and when to let them stay on the back burner. Students have opportunities to use appropriate tools strategically in almost all facets of math class. All you have to do to bring that work to the surface is draw attention to it.

When we do this, we begin to take away the mystery behind the numerous supplies, manipulatives, representations, technology, and mathematical strategies. They'll seem less daunting, and students will learn when each is appropriate to use and how to best use particular tools in particular circumstances. I think back to the *Cake Boss* studio and how lost and overwhelmed I felt when we first started. However, once the instructors helped us understand the functions of the various tools, we began to use the appropriate ones purposefully. We can do the same for our students in math class by valuing the use of tools and taking the time to address how to use them strategically.

CHAPTER 6

Mathematical Practice 6: Attend to Precision

We recently embarked on a major kitchen renovation in my house. I'm talking full-on demolition and reconstruction. As if we weren't crazy enough for tackling this project with four kids in the house, my wife and I also acted as the general contractors for the project (more as a cost-savings measure than a desire to be in charge). Very quickly we realized what a hassle it is trying to be your own GC. Our one-month project turned into a four-month nightmare, and we learned the critical importance of clear and precise communication as we became the conduits between the carpenter, electrician, plumber, and various other subcontractors.

From Day 1 we were thrown into a world of new vocabulary and terminology as we were asked to convey information about four-gang boxes and amperage from our electrician. We relayed messages about compression fittings and backflow preventers from the plumber, all the while understanding very little of what any of it meant. Sometimes the messages were passed without incident. However, when subcontractors had follow-up questions about these messages, they were met by blank stares from us.

What we discovered was that we needed our subcontractors to use precise language that we could understand and communicate to others. We had to ask them to define terms we didn't know and to clarify points that were ambiguous. In addition, my wife and I learned we had to be precise in communicating *our* plans to the subcontractors. We used sketches, photographs, exact measurements, and detailed notes to ensure everyone understood what we wanted. Once we were all on the same page, the project moved forward with fewer mistakes and my wife and

I began recovering our sanity.

The same is true in a mathematics classroom. Math is no longer *only* about "answer getting." Although getting answers is still an integral part of the process, math is not an isolated discipline in which students work in silos independently of their peers. Collaboration and communication are hallmarks of effective math classrooms, and students need to develop the habits and skills necessary for them to successfully convey their ideas to their peers. MP6: Attend to Precision emphasizes that mathematically proficient students must learn to clearly communicate their thinking to others and to themselves.

Throughout this book I have discussed how teachers' roles in the mathematics classroom need to change from being deliverers of content to facilitators of learning. Our students—not us—need to be doing much of the talking. The ideas need to come from them, and that means they need to learn how to communicate their thinking with clear and precise language.

That doesn't mean teachers take a backseat in the process. In the analogy of driving to Boston from Chapter 1, what worked was having a passenger who knew where we were going and would ask me questions to get me thinking about what I needed to do. Instead of telling me where to turn, he would guide my thinking with prompts aimed at activating my prior knowledge. As teachers, we know our rough destination in every math session, but rather than tell students how to get there, we can ask purposeful questions that help move their thinking along.

Knowing how to do this well requires that teachers have a deep understanding of the content and pedagogy associated with primary and elementary mathematics and experience using instructional practices that support this work. Teachers can bolster these areas in many ways, including seeking professional development, reading professional literature, working with instructional coaches or colleagues, and engaging in professional learning communities. As you learn about MP6 and consider how important it is to get students to do the talking in math class, make notes of areas where you would like more experience and use them to help design your own professional learning plan.

Discussing their mathematical thinking is not easy for young students. I think almost every primary-grade teacher has encountered the phrase *I just knew it* when asking students to explain how they arrived at a solution to a problem. Variants of this phrase are *I did it in my head, It just makes sense*, and my favorite, *I used my brain.* Of course, these are all natural responses from young children who have not learned how to communicate the thought process they used as they worked through a problem or task. For many, the fact that they completed the task is good enough. They don't yet understand why they should have to give a play-by-play account of their thinking. Others may lack the ability to give precise descriptions to ariculate their ideas. In any case, it is clear that primary students need a lot of support in this area.

The Elementary Elaboration of MP6 makes this point strongly: "Mathematically proficient students at the elementary grades communicate precisely to others. They start by using everyday language to express their mathematical ideas, realizing that they need to select words with clarity and specificity."

As teachers we know all young students struggle to learn and understand the new language and vocabulary they encounter in each subject. At first this terminology is meaningless to them. Just as I had no idea what a four-gang box was when my electrician asked me to pick up three of them at the supply store, many first graders have no idea what quadrilaterals are.

Kindergartners may refer to an irregular triangle as the pointy shape, first graders may say they "plussed" the numbers when referring to addition, and second graders might refer to the commutative property of addition as "the switch-around rule." This is not unlike what we see in language arts when verbs are referred to as "action words" or in science when students say salt "disappeared" when it dissolved in water. When students move beyond second grade, more emphasis is placed on learning and using correct terminology, but for the purposes of communication in the primary grades, common language and "kid terms" are sufficient and expected.

This makes sense when we think about how students come to understand new mathematical words and concepts. We don't give first graders a list of math vocabulary words with definitions in hopes that they will memorize them and use them correctly in the classroom. We want students exploring ideas to develop conceptual understandings of them. While they explore, they talk with partners and with the class using their own terms. As their understanding grows, they are more receptive to learning terminology. One way this happens is from the teacher using vocabulary in context alongside students' language. When the formal terms are connected to students' language, it helps bridge the conceptual understanding to new vocabulary.

Consider the following example from Ms. Rowell's first-grade class as the students explore features of shapes. As you read the vignette, reflect on the following questions:

Focus Questions

1. How does the teacher support students in learning to use more precise language?
2. How does her choice to allow students to use their own words and terminology help support their work in discussing features of shapes?

Are There Any Other Foxy Shapes?

Ms. Rowell—Grade 1, November

Ms. Rowell gave each pair of students a set of cards containing various regular and irregular polygons to play *Mystery Category*. For this game, students started with all cards faceup on the floor. One student chose a feature of some of the shapes as the mystery category (for example, sides). She then chose one card that fit the category and placed it faceup on the green tray, and one card that didn't fit the category and placed it on the red tray. The partner then chose cards he or she thought fit the category based on the available information and asked if each card fit the category. If it did, it was placed on the green tray. If it didn't, it was placed on the red tray.

This continued until all the shapes were placed on the correct tray. Ms. Rowell had a rule that all the shapes had to be placed for students to guess a category. This encouraged them to consider many features of the shapes and to test out ideas rather than make wild guesses. Once shapes were placed, the guesser could say what she thought the rule was. If she guessed the category correctly, she got a point. If she guessed the category incorrectly, the other student got a point. Students then wrote the category on their whiteboards, which they eventually brought to the whole-group discussion at the end of the session.

Students played the game in pairs for twenty minutes. At the end, Ms. Rowell called them to the floor to share their categories. She was particularly interested in seeing how her first graders would describe the various features of the polygons. She also wanted to get her students talking about features of shapes (numbers of sides, numbers of points, length of sides, and so forth) and learning to clearly communicate their mathematical thinking with each other.

Teacher: I see you all have a number of categories listed on your whiteboards. Who thinks they have one that was kind of challenging?

Trey: Ronit has one. I couldn't get it.

Teacher: Oh really? It sounds like she stumped you. What was it?

Ronit: Foxy shapes.

Teacher: Foxy shapes? That's one I've never heard before. Can you show an example of a foxy shape?

Ronit comes to the document camera and places one shape card for everyone to see (Figure 6.1).

Kendall: Oh, I see it. That's a good one.

Teacher: Can you tell us why it's a foxy shape?

Ronit: 'Cause it looks just like a fox. See the ears and its pointy nose? (Other students nod in agreement.)

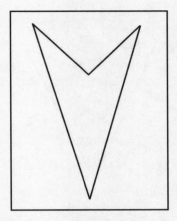

Figure 6.1 Ronit's foxy shape

Teacher: Does anyone have another shape that fits the foxy category?

Ronit: Yeah, a few of them.

Teacher: Let's see if anyone else can find other foxy shapes. Have any of you found another one?

Chase: I think this one is a foxy. (See Figure 6.2.)

Elle: (Laughs.) That's kind of like a skinny foxy. (Others laugh.) Well . . . it is. Look at how pointy and skinny it is.

Tiffany: Yeah, it's like Ronit's, but its ears are squeezed.

Teacher: Are there any other foxy shapes?

Jonah: I think this one is. It's a fat foxy. (See Figure 6.3.)

Teacher: Okay, okay. Can you tell us why it fits the foxy category?

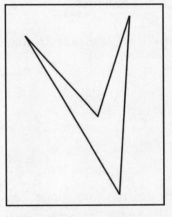

Figure 6.2 Chase's foxy shape

Jonah: It looks like the others, just fatter.

Teacher: Let's look at what we have so far. (See Figures 6.4, 6.5, and 6.6.) You're saying these three shapes all fit the foxy shape category. Why is that? What is the rule for being a foxy? (Some furrowed brows from the students.) What makes a foxy shape a foxy shape? (Hands shoot up.)

Zoe: I think it has to look like a fox.

Teacher: Hmm. I think that's a good starting point,

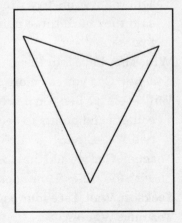

Figure 6.3 Jonah's foxy shape

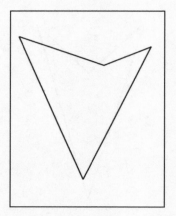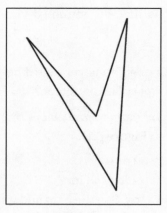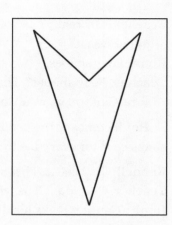

Figures 6.4 a, b, c (Left to right) Comparison of foxy shapes

but I think we need to be more specific. What makes it look like a fox?

Zoe: (Shrugs.) I don't know. It just does.

Teacher: Can you talk about the parts of the shape that seem important for foxy shapes?

Zoe: Um . . . It has pointy ears?

Teacher: How many? Can you be more specific?

Zoe: Two. A foxy has two pointy ears.

Ronit: And one pointy nose.

Teacher: So how many pointy parts does a foxy have?

Ronit: Three.

Teacher: I'm going to write this down—kind of like a definition of a foxy shape. You said they have three pointy parts? Is there anything else that's important with foxies?

Will: They have four lines.

Teacher: Can you say more about that?

Will: Well, it's like you need to . . . It's like . . . Can I come up? (Walks to the document camera and points to each side and counts.) See, they each have four lines: one, two, three, four.

Teacher: Can we add that to our definition? A foxy has three pointy parts and is made with four lines. How does that sound? (Heads nod in agreement.)

Jackson: Wait, I see four pointy parts.

Teacher: Where?

Jackson: Right here (points to the middle of one shape). It's like the . . . what do you call it?

Ronit: Eyebrows.

Jackson: No, it's like the top. Not hair (points to the top of his head). Like this.

Ronit: His head?

Jackson: I guess.

Teacher: Okay, how do we feel about changing our rule for foxy shapes? We'll change the three pointy parts to four pointy parts. Is there anything different about the pointy part Jackson pointed out?

Jonah: It goes down. It's like pointy going down.

Ronit: But this (points to the nose of the foxy shape) goes down too.

Jonah: Oh.

Jackson: Wait! It's different. It's like a dent. His head got smushed. (Laughter from the class.)

Teacher: The dent is different than the other three pointy parts?

Jackson: Yes, it goes in.

Teacher: Can we say foxies have three pointy parts on the outside and one pointy part that goes in? How does that sound? (Agreement from the group.) And then we said they have four lines. Hmm. Does anyone know what we call the straight lines of a shape?

Chase: Sides?

Teacher: Yes, we call them sides. I noticed some of you using that word in your categories today. I'm going to put this in parentheses in our definition. (Have four sides.) So we can say foxies are made with four lines or we can say they have four sides. They also have four points.

Ronit: Like a square.

Teacher: Yes, squares also have four sides and four points.

Jonah: So do rectangles.

Teacher: True, those have four sides and four points as well. What makes a foxy different from a square or rectangle?

Zoe: They look like foxes.

Jackson: They have dents.

Teacher: So it looks like we know about three kinds of shapes that have four sides and four points. We have another name for shapes that fit this rule called quadrilaterals. It's kind of a big word and you don't need to worry about using it yet, but I wanted you to know that.

Ms. Rowell shifted the discussion to other categories and had similar discussions with her students. Some of their categories were specific defining attributes (six sides, three corners, and so on) whereas others were nondefining attributes (such as skinny and long). As students provided examples, Ms. Rowell encouraged them to use specific words to explain why they thought certain shapes fit the category, all the while supporting students to attend to precision.

This is a good example of a teacher encouraging students to use their own words to talk about features of two-dimensional shapes. There was no need to expect students to know and use a term such as *concave quadrilateral* in this session focused on describing features of shape. Merely referring to that kind of shape as a "foxy" worked because she had students describe its features and develop a working definition of a "foxy" shape. In the end, once students worked to describe features using their own words, she introduced the term *quadrilateral*. It wasn't the focal point of the lesson, but offering precise terms in conjunction with student-developed terminology helps students connect their own understanding with new vocabulary.

Students practiced using precise descriptors with support from their teacher. The specific questions Ms. Rowell asked helped them attend to the precision of their language:

"How many? Can you be more specific?"

"Can you say more about that?"

"I think that's a good starting point, but I think we need to be more specific."

"Does anyone know what we call the straight lines of a shape?"

"Can you talk about the parts of the shape that seem important?"

In most cases, Ms. Rowell prompted students to provide more information about each shape. This is an important kind of prompt, because young students aren't predisposed to offer thorough and complete responses. They need encouragement and support as they learn how to be precise in their communication. Also, Ms. Rowell offered very little information in the discussion and really worked to encourage students to build off each other's thinking. She supported individual students to be more detailed while supporting the whole class by creating a collective definition using everyone's ideas.

Ms. Rowell also supported students by introducing more formal vocabulary to connect with their own terminology. They had been referring to the sides of the foxy shape as lines. There's nothing wrong with that since there are four lines that make up these shapes. However, she chose to use the opportunity to introduce the term *side*. I asked her about it after the session:

> A few of my students were using the word *side* to describe shapes, but most just called them lines. I wanted to introduce the word, but I didn't want to simply force it on them and have it be disconnected from their work. This discussion provided just the opportunity I was looking for, because we were coming up with different words to describe shapes. I give students the option of using either *side* or *line* when describing their shapes, but eventually we'll all just use the term *side*.

This is a great example of connecting more formal language to students' vernacular. It was a low-pressure situation and Ms. Rowell offered up another way of describing something. She also included the word in the whole-class definition list they were creating so students could see it written. She gave students the option of using either word, but also had the expectation that eventually they would all use the word *side*.

All primary-grade teachers can support students in attending to precision by encouraging them to be explicit in the ways they describe their thinking, justifications, generalizations, and reasoning. Ask follow-up questions and probe students for more information. Help them to see when they are being ambiguous and vague, and support them as they try to be more precise in their explanations. Also know that there are times when it's okay to give students a word they are searching for.

Supporting students' work on precision involves letting them muddle around with their own vocabulary and language. This helps students learn to use language and terms that make sense to their peers. However, we ultimately want them to learn and use more precise language. Knowing when it's okay to have students use everyday language and when more mathematical language is preferred comes down to the mathematical goals for particular student(s) in any given session.

To illustrate this point, the following example demonstrates a time when it was appropriate for a teacher to offer a specific term to develop a student's ability to be more precise. This comes from a second-grade classroom where a student was trying to describe a conjecture about what was happening in this series of equations:

$$6 + 6 = 12 \qquad 4 + 6 = 10 \qquad 15 + 15 = 30 \qquad 22 + 28 = 50$$

$$6 + 7 = 13 \qquad 4 + 7 = 11 \qquad 16 + 15 = 31 \qquad 23 + 28 = 51$$

Each series of equations shows one being added to an addend and the sum increasing by one. Mr. Tankersley was working to help his students make conjectures about addition-based regularity they noticed (MP8).

Teacher: What are you noticing about all these equations?

Jenessa: They're just adding . . . They're just adding one more to one of the addends.

Teacher: Thanks for using the word *addend*. It's helpful in letting us know which part of the equation you're referring to. (A huge, genuine smile breaks out on Jenessa's face.) And you said each of these equations has one being added to one of the addends? (She nods.) Did you notice anything else?

Jenessa: It's adding one more to the addends and it's just putting one more onto the (a slight pause) to the answer? (A longer pause.) To the expression. (I could tell she was searching for a vocabulary word we had used in class when working on our other general statements. She began to write her idea on the paper I had given her.)

Teacher: And it looks to me like you were searching for that word *sum*.

Jenessa: Sum. Yeah. I couldn't get it. (Again, a smile, this time of relief.)

Teacher: Yeah, I know. I could tell that's the word you were searching for, because sometimes people call the sums in an addition problem "the answer."

In this case, we see a student who was struggling to find the right word. She knew it was the answer and was trying to think of the correct mathematical term. After a few failed attempts the teacher provided her with the word. These opportunities to introduce more formal terminology present themselves at different times for different students. A second grader still working on developing addition strategies that go beyond counting all might not need to focus his attention on the terminology of addends and sums. However, for Janessa, who was working on a conjecture that adding one to an addend would increase the sum by the same amount, those words were incredibly helpful.

Clear communication is a big part of effective math classrooms and a big focus of MP6. As students explore concepts and develop ideas, their need for more formal language grows. It's a natural process that can be supported if teachers create classrooms that promote open discourse and debate. The more students talk about math with the support of their teachers, the more they develop their skills of precise communication.

I cannot stress enough the importance of developing a classroom community that supports students' talking about their mathematical ideas. This may be a big shift for many teachers, and it takes time, but if teachers truly want to support the work of MP6 and the other MPs, then they need the shift to happen. One way to assess the degree to which you support students' voices in your classroom is to re-cord yourself as you teach. When you watch or listen to the recording, take note of how much you talk and how much the students do. Also, pay attention to what you are saying. Are you asking open-ended questions that elicit more responses from students? Do you ask students to clarify their own thinking or do you do it for them by restating what they say? This process can tell you whether you need to shift your practice significantly.

The second part of MP6 deals with students' use of symbols and their under-standing of them. The Elementary Elaborations (Illustrative Mathematics 2014) say, "Elementary students learn to use mathematical symbols correctly and can describe the meaning of the symbols they use. In particular, they understand that the equal sign denotes that two quantities have the same value, and can use it flexibly to express equivalences. For example, the equivalence of 8 and 5 + 3 can be written both as 5 + 3 = 8 and 8 = 5 + 3. Similarly, the equivalence of 6 + 2 and 5 + 3 is expressed as 6 + 2 = 5 + 3."

It is important for students to learn what mathematical symbols represent and to have a deep understanding of the mathematics related to them. Here are a few symbols that our elementary students encounter and are expected to use in the primary grades:

Addition	+
Subtraction	−
Equal	=
Strict Inequality (Greater-Than and Less-Than)	> <

I find it helpful to see this list because it makes the symbolic portion of MP6 seem very manageable. We focus on only a small number of symbols in the primary grades: the addition, subtraction, and equal signs, and to a lesser extent the "great-er-than" and "less-than" symbols. The mathematical ideas behind these symbols are complex, and students need lots of experiences making sense of them and connecting that thinking to the symbols.

If the goal is to have students learn to use mathematical symbols correctly and be able to describe their meaning, then it is important that they have lots of opportunities to develop an understanding of the mathematics that underlie them. Students should learn that operation symbols are more than just an instruction to do something to the numbers. The expression 5 + 3 actually describes the relationship of the values. There is one group of 5 and one group of 3. The + sign conveys that these two groups are being combined. *Combining, joining, putting together*, and so on are ways to describe both the relationship between the addends in this expression and the action of addition.

As students have rich experiences that help them make sense of addition, their knowledge, understanding, and use of the addition sign becomes more meaningful. The symbol becomes a more precise way for them to represent their mathematical reasoning in addition. Rather than express their reasoning to solve 12 + 6 by writing, *First I broke apart the 12 into a 10 and a 2. Then I added 2 and 6 together to make 8. Then I added the 8 to 10 to make 18*, students can write the following:

$$12 + 6 = \underline{\quad}$$

$$12 = 10 + 2$$

$$6 + 2 = 8$$

$$8 + 10 = 18$$

Particular emphasis of MP6 is on the equal sign, and rightfully so. Lots of students learn that the equal sign means "Here comes the answer" or "Put the answer next to this." Textbooks often reinforce this by presenting problems that have the equal sign only at the end. When students experience the equal sign like this, they miss the idea that it is describing the equivalence of two or more values.

One way teachers can support students' understanding of the equal sign and equivalence is to present various equations and problems that flexibly incorporate the equal sign. Instead of writing *12 + 6 =* ____ for students to solve, try presenting it as ____ *= 12 + 6*. If your students have not had experiences with equations written with the sum as the initial value, this equation might surprise them. Don't be shocked if you get some pushback. In fact, discussions that result from pushing students' conceptualizations can often be quite powerful, as seen in this next vignette written by Ms. Ammarell about her first-grade students discussing the equal sign.

‖ Focus Questions

1. How does Ms. Ammarell's decision not to explicitly teach the meaning of the equal sign support the students' work with MP6?
2. What role does Ms. Ammarell play during this exchange?
3. What next steps could she take to support the development of the ideas presented in this exchange?

You Can't Write It That Way

Ms. Ammarell—Grade 1, May

My first graders had been working for quite some time with a variety of scenarios involving addition. We played games that use addition, solved story problems with addition, and did number work with addition. Each time my students saw addition situations expressed with numbers, the equal sign was always at the end of the equation. I was curious what my students actually thought about the equal sign and how they made sense of it, so I decided to push on this idea a bit.

The students were working on the following story problem:

‖ **SAM SAW 4 RED FISH AND 3 ORANGE FISH IN THE POND. HOW MANY FISH DID HE SEE?**

All of the students wrote the equation as either *4 + 3 = 7* or *3 + 4 = 7*. I called the class to the floor and wrote the two equations the students used on our chart paper.

Teacher: I noticed that as we worked today, there were two different ways students in the class wrote the number sentence for the problem. Raise your hand if you wrote it this way. (Points to 4 + 3 = 7, and most students raise their hands.) Okay, now raise your hand if you wrote it the other way. (The rest put their hands up.) Is there any other way we could write that equation?

There was a brief pause, as the students considered my question, and plenty of looks of uncertainty. I was hesitant to offer more clarification of my question because I really wanted to see what their ideas were and feared I would guide them too much if I was too explicit.

Shamel: Do you mean like with words?

Teacher: Can you say more about what you mean?

Shamel: Like can you spell it? You know, like write *f-o-r* and then you write *plus* and then spell three. Like write it out.

Teacher: Yeah, we could certainly write it our with words. That's another way. Any other ideas?

Katie: Can you show it with pictures?

Teacher: Hmmm. Can you explain a bit more about that?

Katie: What if you draw . . . say . . . three circles and then put a plus mark and then four more circles? (Pauses.) And then put equals and then seven circles.

Teacher: Sure. That could be another way. These are interesting ideas. I'm wondering if there is a way we could write the equation using numbers. (There's another brief pause.)

Luke: One plus 1 plus 1 plus 1 plus 1 plus 1 . . . (Looks at his fingers.) Plus 1 plus 1 equals 7.

Teacher: That works as another way to write this, but I'm wondering if we can re-write the number sentence using the numbers we already have.

Jordan: How about 7 equals 4 plus 3? Can we do that?

Brandon: No, that makes no sense.

Jessica: Yeah it does.

Teacher: Let's talk about this. Brandon, why do you say it makes no sense? Can you explain your thinking?

Brandon: 'Cause the equals has to come at the end. It doesn't look right that way.

Tyler: It's backward.

Teacher: Jessica, you seem to agree with Jordan; can you say more?

Jessica: It's just the same thing: 7 is the same as 4 plus 3.

Jordan: Yeah, it's the same either way.

I notice that the majority of the students are unsure but are listening intently to the debate. Brandon and Tyler seem adamant that it can't be written the way Jordan suggests, and Jessica and Jordan are sure of their thinking. I decide to push them toward defining what the equal sign means.

Teacher: What does the equal sign mean?

Tyler: It tells you where to put the answer.

Jessica: No, it means it's the same. (She gets up and points to the first equation on the chart.) See, 4 and 3 is the same as 7. It's the same thing.

Teacher: If I write it like this (writes $7 = 4 + 3$), how would you read that?

Jessica: Seven is the same as 4 and 3.

Brandon: I don't know . . . it's . . . it looks wrong.

Teacher: Are you saying it is wrong or it looks wrong?

Bradon: It just looks wrong. I'm not really sure.

Teacher: How many of you think we can write it this way? (About half the hands go up.) I know it looks weird because you're used to seeing it written with the equal sign at the end. However, Jessica and Jordan are onto something with their idea about equal meaning the same as. We'll keep exploring this idea as we continue to work with our number sentences.

If students are to learn what symbols mean and how to use them correctly, they need a lot of opportunities to talk explicitly about the mathematics behind the symbols and the symbols themselves. One observation from this vignette is that Ms. Ammarell made no assumptions about student understanding. She required students to explain their thinking or articulate their confusion. In this exchange they were exposed to an idea that the equal sign can be used differently from the way they had previously experienced it. Very few students owned that idea, but that's how these big understandings begin. An idea surfaces, students play around with it for a while and discuss their thinking, and then the idea begins to grow and take hold.

Ms. Ammarell could have used this as an opportunity to tell the students the equal sign conveys equivalence and that they could place it in various positions. However, they would have just learned that fact based on her authority rather than on what makes sense based on their experience. By allowing students to discuss their understandings and confusions about this concept, Ms. Ammarell was able to get them thinking about what made sense and what was still confusing. She considered what they said during the course of the discussion and asked clarifying questions to help her students attend to precision as they communicated their mathematical thinking for their classmates. The idea that the equal sign conveys equivalence was one that needed time to develop, and one conversation was not going to be enough.

This session was an initial opportunity to raise important ideas. In an effort to get more clarification, she worked to call on students who had been thinking about what the equal sign meant. This revealed some understanding, but also lots of confusion. Students had assumptions about the symbols and where they belonged, and now those assumptions were being challenged. The disequilibrium is important in helping students shift their thinking. They are seeking to make sense of this idea and are invested in exploring it. She mentioned that this idea would get revisited often over the next few weeks.

Some next steps for Ms. Ammarell's class could be to work on some problems that are written differently (for example, ___ = 14 + 4 or 9 + 3 = 8 + ___). This exposure would provide more experience with different structures and also give students a reason to talk about the equal sign and what it means. She could also try a routine called *Ways to Make* where students are presented with a sum and have to come up with various expressions that total that sum. Rather than leave it open-ended, she could create a sheet with a series of equations that look like this: 11 = ___ + ___. She could also present contexts where students work on both-addends-unknown situations. (For example, Jason has eleven pieces of candy. Some are chocolate and some are lollipops. What is one combination of candy that he could have?) Finally, she could have students use cubes to explore the idea of equivalence and connect this cube representation to the symbolic representation.

Each of these options for next steps provides opportunities to expose students to alternative structures for problems and push on the idea that the equal sign conveys equivalence. More importantly, they provide chances to have conversations around this idea. With more exposure to these structures and more opportunities to discuss these ideas, the students will work toward a great collective understanding of the meaning behind the equal sign, which gets at the heart of this aspect of MP6.

A final component of MP6 is the idea of students being precise in their mathematical work. The Elementary Elaborations from Illustrative Mathematics (2014) say the following:

> From Kindergarten on, they count accurately, using strategies so that they include each object once and only once without losing track. Mathematically proficient students calculate accurately and efficiently and use clear and concise notation to record their work.

Whether counting, solving problems, or measuring an object, mathematically proficient students work carefully to minimize the chances that they'll make an error. They work to have accurate answers and practice using the most concise and clear forms of notation. This aspect of MP6 is the most familiar to teachers because there has always been an emphasis on accuracy in mathematics.

Primary students are new to this notion of accuracy. Before formal schooling, much of their mathematical experience has been exploratory and without too much emphasis on making accurate calculations or counting quantities without error. Although we certainly maintain a good amount of exploration in mathematics to support their growth, development, and interest in math, we also introduce more occasions where accuracy matters.

There is an entire skill set associated with accuracy. Students need to pay attention to minute details regardless of the task they're engaged in. If it involves counting, they carefully organize objects to ensure that each is counted only once and that they haven't missed any. If they are building geometric designs out of blocks, they carefully place individual blocks to align edges appropriately so they create an accurate shape. When problem solving, they count or calculate accurately and efficiently while taking time to check over their work.

Skills that support accuracy need to be developed and practiced often throughout students' experiences in school. Teachers can support this work by using formative assessments aimed at assessing not only students' accuracy, but also the skills they use as they work on tasks. For example, having students count a bag of cubes independently and then put a total on a sheet of paper can give you an indication of their accuracy. However, observing a student count the cubes from the bag can tell you much more. Did the student organize the cubes before counting? Did she demonstrate one-to-one correspondence? Did she check her count or count the set only once? This information tells you not only if a student can count accurately, but also how she goes about counting and what skills she still needs to develop.

There is power in this type of formative assessment. If you placed a pile of twenty-four cubes on a table in a kindergarten class early in the school year and asked each student to count them, what would you observe? We certainly wouldn't expect to see all students strategically place them in organized groups and count them a few times to ensure they had the correct amount. More likely we would see a range of approaches, with some students focusing more closely on getting an accurate count and others struggling to keep track of their counting.

Mr. Moll does this exact counting activity as a formative assessment with his kindergartners each year to get a sense of their counting strategies. Below are some of his recorded observations from December. As you read through his notes, consider what skills students are demonstrating and what areas they might need to develop.

Mary Anne	She took one cube at a time and counted them as she placed them on the other side of the table. When she got to twelve, she realized she had skipped eleven, pushed them all back, and started again. This time she counted faster and at times actually counted two numbers as she moved one cube over. Her total was twenty-eight.
Eve	She dumped the whole bag out and organized them by color. She then proceeded to count them by ones. She did this very methodically by focusing on one color at a time. She accurately counted twenty-four. Without prompting, she went back and counted them again, confirming twenty-four as her count.
Heather	She counted by touching each cube but did not move the cubes or try to rearrange them. As a result she counted many more than once. She said there were thirty-two cubes.
Ting	He removed one cube at a time out of the bag while counting each one aloud. This seemed rather easy for him. He very quickly counted twenty-four cubes. When asked if he wanted to check his count, he said he didn't need to. He was sure it was twenty-four.
Efran	He used his pointer finger to point to individual cubes as he counted. There did not appear to be an order in which he counted, and he frequently counted the same cube more than once. He counted accurately up to fourteen and then just repeated fourteen over and over as he counted.

As we see in these examples (and know from experience) students do not come prewired to focus on accuracy. They need to develop skills and strategies to help them count, calculate, measure, and draw accurately. They also need to learn to value the importance of this kind of precision. Heather, Ting, and Efran were satisfied with their count and did not see a need to go back and recount or check their work. Mary Anne recognized she had made an error early in her counting and started again. She made another counting error during her second attempt but did not catch it and did not count the set another time.

We support young students in developing the skills and appreciation of accuracy by being explicit about its importance. Students tend to follow their teacher's lead. If he or she seems to care about how carefully they are counting or calculating, they will begin to pay attention to these details as they work. The following vignette from Mr. Moll's class explores the issue of careful counting. This exchange happened the day after completing the counting assessment above.

‖ Focus Questions

1. How does Mr. Moll use the information from his formative assessment to guide this discussion with students?
2. How does he support students in thinking about the importance of accuracy?

Careful Counting

Mr. Moll—Kindergarten, December

I recently conducted an assessment of all my kindergartners to get a sense of how their counting was developing. I gave them twenty-four cubes and asked them to count them. As they did this, I took notes about their behaviors to get a sense of how well they could count and what aspects of counting were not yet evident. Not surprisingly, quite a few had difficulty getting an accurate count. A large number of my students can orally count fairly high for this point in the year (above thirty), but when counting objects, many tend to get disorganized and lose track of what they have already counted. I wanted to address this issue with them and give them an activity to practice counting accurately.

Rather than having me show them effective counting strategies or tell them what to do, I wanted to have a conversation with them about why it's important to count accurately. I wanted the ideas to come from them so they would have ownership of them. I knew some students had good strategies and planned to have them contribute some ideas to the group. Here's how the conversation went:

Teacher: We've been doing a lot of work this year practicing our counting. Why do you think we do that? Why should we practice counting?

Ting: So we get good at it.

Teacher: Why is that important?

Heather: For when we need things and you have to have just that many . . . Like if you need 3 eggs, you need to count 3 of them so you don't have 2 or 1 or 10.

Teacher: Like if we were making a cake. Who likes cake? (Hands shoot up.) So you're saying that if we needed 3 eggs for the recipe, you need to make sure you count out 3 eggs so you don't have too many or not enough?

Heather: Yeah. My mom lets me crack the eggs.

Teacher: That's awesome. Ting said we need to practice so we get better at counting, and Heather said we need to get better at counting so we can make sure we have the right number of things like eggs. How do you all make sure you are counting carefully? What does careful counting look like?

Efran: You go slow, like 1 . . . 2 . . . 3 . . .

Teacher: Okay, so we count slowly. I'm going to write that down on this chart and we'll call it "Careful Counting." What else do we do?

Eve: I do it a bunch of times. I count them and then count them and then count them.

Teacher: So you count something once and then count it again to make sure you get the same amount?

Eve: Uh-huh (smiling).

Teacher: I'll write that down too. This idea was one I didn't see from everybody as you counted with me. Some of you counted more than once, but many of you counted just one time. Is this something we can all try to do? (Heads nod.) Good. Anything else we want to add to the list? (Silence.) What if we have a pile of cubes all bunched up like we had when you each counted with me? How would you count them carefully?

Mary Anne: I moved them. Like 1, 2, 3 (miming the action of moving cubes from one pile to the next).

Teacher: You touch each thing being counted and move it away from the things that aren't counted yet?

Mary Anne: Yes, and you have to move it far away so they don't get mixed up.

(Kids were getting restless.)

Teacher: Okay, I'll write that last one down in two parts: touch each thing you count, and keep track of what you count.

Careful Counting

1. Count slowly
2. Check your counting
3. Touch each thing you count
4. Keep track

We reviewed the list one more time, and then I sent the students to their tables to work on a counting bag activity with their math partners. Each pair of students had a bag with a set of objects in it. They were instructed to count the objects in the bag using the careful counting strategies we talked about as a group. Kindergarten students need lots of practice with counting, but it also helps to make the notion of precision very explicit. We have a lot of work ahead of us, but I think we're off to a great start.

The above example demonstrates how a teacher can support students in attending to precision by addressing the importance of accuracy and developing effective strategies for counting, measuring, and calculating. Mr. Moll used a formative assessment to get a sense of where his students were with regard to counting, identified some issues, and then had a conversation with his students so they could address the issues collectively.

It seemed to him that many students weren't being particularly careful when it came to keeping track of the cubes when counting. The notion of "careful counting" is important, and he decided to address it in the form of a class discussion to get different students talking about what works for them and what they need to pay attention to when trying to get accurate counts. During the discussion, one student raised a strategy of recounting, and Mr. Moll used the opportunity to address this issue with the class. He wanted to see more students double-checking their count and used Mary Anne's suggestion as a way to highlight this point.

Throughout the discussion, Mr. Moll asked lots of questions to get his students talking, which supports the idea of giving ownership to the students. As Mr. Moll said, he chose not to tell students how to count. Instead he asked them why it was important to count carefully and then asked them what that looked like. As a result, the list of strategies came from the students and was more meaningful to them because they had to construct that knowledge.

Teachers can facilitate conversations about how their students attend to precision by asking them to discuss what they pay attention to when they're trying to be accurate. Students have strategies and ideas to share, and with practice, they can articulate them to their classmates. We can support them by asking clarifying questions like Mr. Moll did during this discussion. The key is to know which ideas and skills are important and which students are demonstrating them.

Although one element of precision talks about exact answers, a larger part of this practice standard addresses how precisely students communicate their mathematical ideas. Often students need to talk with others to explain their reasoning behind an approach to a math task or a conjecture they make. Other times, they might have to articulate why a particular math solution is correct or incorrect. This communication is not limited to verbal expression. Students can articulate their reasoning through writing, through representations, or with numbers and symbols.

Attending to precision as they communicate mathematical thinking can be quite challenging for young students. When students move beyond second grade, the need for precision may require more formal language, as well as understandings of mathematical concepts, symbols, and definitions. Primary students, on the other hand, are just beginning to learn all of these things, so it's important to recognize that the level of precision with which they communicate is going to be lower than what we'd expect from older elementary students.

It's our responsibility as primary teachers to help students recognize the importance of attending to precision. We can work to create classrooms that encourage, support, and expect students to communicate mathematical ideas; to value this form of communication and help students see the need to be clear and precise; and to dedicate time to exploring what symbols mean so students have a conceptual understanding of the mathematics behind them. And finally we can help students recognize the importance of working carefully, focusing on details, and being precise in their counting, calculating, and measuring.

Developing our students' appreciation of precision will prepare them for future success in mathematics. Primary teachers set the tone for all subjects. Students develop a sense of what reading, writing, science, social studies, and math classes are like from their experience in K–2 classrooms. They learn how these instructional periods function and how they are expected to behave and interact through their experiences in our classrooms. Learning about the importance of precision from Day 1 will stay with them as they progress through school.

CHAPTER 7

Mathematical Practice 7: Look For and Make Use of Structure

One of my favorite movies of all time is *The Matrix*. I love the action, I love the suspense, and I love the connection it has with MP7. *The Matrix* is about a man named Neo who finds out that the world he thought he lived in was just a computerized world called the Matrix created by robots to control humans. He has spent his whole life immersed in this highly structured world, completely unaware of living in a computer program. That is, until a man named Morpheus unplugs him from the system and opens his eyes to the reality of it. With the support of Morpheus, Neo embarks on a long series of training sessions to learn about and understand the hidden structures of the Matrix so he can use them to his advantage.

After completing his training, he returns to the Matrix so he can help free others. He uses his greater understanding of the structure of the system to exploit it and do amazing superhero-like moves, such as run up walls, dodge bullets, and even fly. Essentially, as a result of learning how the Matrix works, he can do much more than anyone who is still plugged in to the system.

Math is very much like the Matrix. It is full of structure. There are structures in the way our number system is organized. There are structures in the properties and behaviors of the operations. There are structures in the way geometric shapes are constructed. And like Neo in the beginning of the movie, students can interact in this mathematical world without really knowing about or understanding the intricacies of these structures. In essence, they can have a very limited worldview of mathematics. However, if students are provided opportunities to explore the structures in meaningful ways, they can exploit them just like Neo does.

Consider Keisha, a second grader who spent a lot of time in class exploring the behavior of subtraction with her teacher, Ms. Adams. I was observing her class one day at the end of May when they were working on a subtraction problem. Ms. Adams presented the problem 85 – 37 and asked students to solve it using any strategy they preferred. In just a few moments, Keisha proudly raised her hand, indicating that she was already finished. When I walked over to see what she had done, she said eagerly, "I changed the problem to make it easier. I knew you needed to add 3 to 37 to make 40, and I knew if I did the same thing to 85, it would give me a new problem with the same answer. So I added 3 to 85 and got 88. Now it's 88 minus 40, which equals 48."

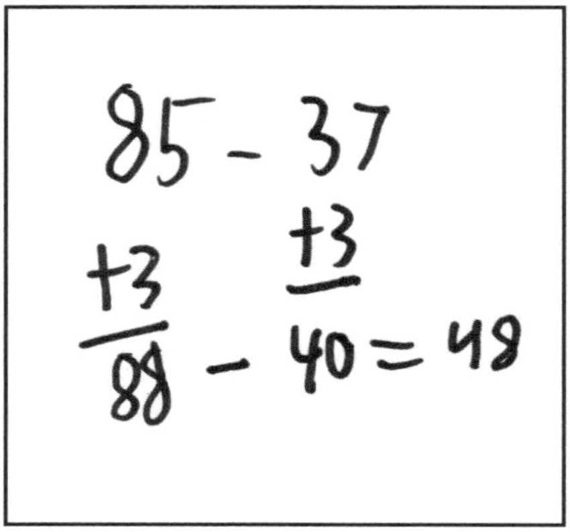

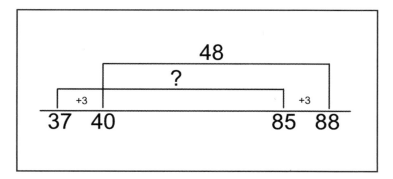

$$85 - 37$$
$$+3 \qquad +3$$
$$\overline{88} - 40 = 48$$

Figure 7.1 Keisha's recording of her thinking

I asked her to record her thinking so I could see how she conceptualized it. Her work is shown in Figure 7.1.

I was quite impressed with her reasoning and the fact that she could hold all that in her head. Upon further conversation with Keisha, I learned that she had become so comfortable with the structure of subtraction and the fact that if you change both the minuend and the subtrahend by the same amount, the difference will remain the same, that she had focused on only one small aspect of the problem. She said, "I was just trying to make zeros in the second number. Once I figured out I needed 3 more, I just did 85 plus 3 to get 88, and then it was easy. Eighty minus 40 is 40. Then it's just 8 more to 48."

Keisha used her understanding of the base ten structure of numbers and the structure of subtraction to apply a generalized rule she and her classmates discovered and developed. She wanted the subtrahend to end in a zero to make it a problem she could do in her head. She added 3 to 37, but to keep the difference the same, she had to add 3 to 85 as well. We can see this more easily on a number line (Figure 7.2).

Figure 7.2 Number line representation

Keisha was trying to calculate the distance between 37 and 85, but those numbers made the mental calculation complicated. In order to simplify it, she added 3 to 37 to make a nice friendly number (40), but in doing so, she shrank the distance between the two original numbers. To compensate for it, she had to add 3 to 85. This kept the distance between the two values the same so that when she solved her new problem, the answer was equivalent to the original problem.

This idea that she can create new equivalent problems became very easy for her as a result of her work exploring the structure of subtraction. Students often notice ways in which addition and subtraction behave when they play around with different ideas, and some even develop and use such strategies on their own. Sometimes they have a deep understanding of why a certain strategy works, and other times they just know it as a pattern that has worked every time they try it. Teachers can support students by encouraging a more purposeful exploration to deepen their understanding of the mathematical structures behind these efficient strategies.

Ms. Adams did just that with her students. Keisha and her classmates worked for some time exploring how subtraction problems were affected by changing certain elements. As a result, Keisha developed a generalization about how she could alter subtraction problems to make equivalent problems, and using her understanding of the tens-and-ones structure of whole numbers, she could choose her numbers strategically to apply the approach quickly and accurately. This is an example of a student making use of structure, and it shows the power behind this standard for mathematical practice.

Keisha's reasoning was a result of an accumulation of many experiences she and her classmates had purposefully exploring the structure of subtraction and the base ten structure of numbers with the support of her teacher. She wasn't applying a rule her teacher had showed the class one day. She owned this idea because she was given time and specific mathematical tasks that helped her see the structure of subtraction and develop an understanding of how this particular operation behaved. A full vignette from Ms. Adams's class appears at the end of the chapter and gives a glimpse of the class's earlier work with subtraction.

The goal of this chapter is to provide you with an understanding of the kinds of structures primary-grade students encounter and strategies you can use to help students look for and make use of those structures. This work can have powerful effects on students' mathematical reasoning. Once we learn to recognize when opportunities to explore structure arise, we can decide how best to bring these ideas to the surface with our students.

More often than not, our work around MP7 in the primary grades is subtle and spontaneous because it emerges from the work our students do in the moment. When we notice students using structures, we can simply ask them about it as a way to draw their attention to the fact that there is something important about those ideas.

By commenting on or questioning a student's work with structure, a teacher helps the student recognize that she or he did something important. It also alerts other students to look for the same or related structures. Also, if the teacher comments on the same structure at different times, students can see that structure in different contexts. Note that naming and commenting on structure in context doesn't take more than a few seconds: "Tim used tens to solve this problem. He has been thinking a lot about tens lately."

Other times teachers may decide they want to unpack this work more deeply, so they design tasks and explorations that focus on a particular structure like Ms. Adams did. These explorations can last for one class period or go on for days, depending on the interest of the students. As teachers we can decide how we want to address these ideas, when we want to address them, and for how long. Supporting MP7 really comes down to this:

- Recognizing when students are working on an idea connected to structure and bringing the idea to the surface through questions and comments
- Giving students opportunities to see and explore a structure in their own work or in tasks designed to highlight particular structures
- Providing time for students to build an understanding of it
- Supporting students as they apply their knowledge of the structure in novel tasks

It is important to note that teachers and students do not need to name all the underlying mathematics to be able to see and use structure. Many structures are easy to recognize, even if they aren't always easy to express. Kindergartners notice very early in their math work that when they add zero to a quantity, the amount does not change (5 + 0 = 5). Although they apply this idea in their daily work, it's safe to say they aren't thinking about it as the additive-identity property (nor should they).

In another example, shown in Figure 7.3, a first grader named Pratima added a string of numbers and noticed she did not have to add them in order and instead could strategically group them to make the calculation easier.

Pratima is making use of structure (the base ten structure of numbers and the commutative and associative properties of addition) but in no way is expected to

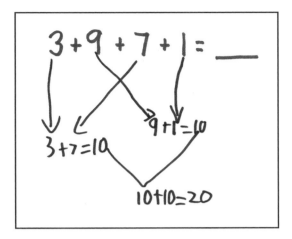

Figure 7.3 Pratima's strategy for adding a string of numbers

articulate these properties in a formal sense. For young students, it is enough to talk about these structures using familiar language. She may comment that she can add the numbers by chunking together familiar pairs and get the same total as she would by adding the numbers in order from left to right. MP7 is not about naming the structures; it's about seeing them and making use of them.

As I mentioned earlier, supporting MP7 requires us to recognize when students are working with mathematical ideas that are built around structure. So how do we know when this is happening? Put simply, ideas that can be generalized and applied in novel situations are built on structure. Following are some examples to help clarify this point.

As we saw in Pratima's example, students might notice that when they change the order of the addends in an addition expression, the sum remains the same. They can substitute lots of different numbers and experiment with this idea, and it will always work. When they deepen their understanding of this idea, they will eventually be able to make general statements such as "You can switch the numbers around in an addition problem and the answer always stays the same." When students make general claims like this, it is evidence that they are beginning to understand particular structures related to the operation of addition.

For another example, consider the following two story problems.

> THREE CHILDREN ON THE PLAYGROUND ARE PLAYING TAG. FOUR CHILDREN ARE ON THE STRUCTURE. HOW MANY CHILDREN ARE ON THE PLAYGROUND?
>
> NIRA FOUND THREE PENCILS ON THE FLOOR AND FOUR PENCILS ON THE ART TABLE. HOW MANY PENCILS DID NIRA FIND?

A child who counts to determine that there are seven children on the playground and then announces, "I know Nira found seven pencils because it's the same as the first problem," recognizes the common mathematical structure between the two problems and makes use of the structure to solve the second problem.

A child who calculates 8 + 6 by saying, "8 plus 2 is 10 and 4 more is 14" knows that, to add two numbers, an addend can be decomposed and added in parts. She decomposes the 6 in order to make a 10 because she knows how to add any single-digit number to 10. That is, she makes use of a structure of addition as well as the structure of teen numbers.

When a kindergartner notices that she can make many different rectangles using square tiles or when she keeps using two red trapezoids to create hexagons, she is making use of the structure of how particular geometric shapes are composed.

In all of these examples, the students' ideas can be applied in new situations and will work consistently. When we can generalize a mathematical idea, it is rooted in structure. Take some time to consider the mathematical work you and your students explore during the year. What ideas surface that are generalizable? Exploring this question will help you develop a lens to recognize opportunities to investigate structure with your students.

We help our students engage in MP7 by giving them opportunities to discover and explore structures so they can begin to apply their understanding of them in new contexts. As we saw with Keisha, once students understand a structure and why it works, it strengthens their mathematical reasoning. The whole point of this work is to help students learn to make use of structures to their advantage.

As with all the mathematical practices, there are no standardized teaching methods to help students look for and make use of structure. Opportunities for this work will surface frequently in the natural flow of a math class. You just need to be on the lookout for those moments when structures are evident and then capitalize on them.

A great way to begin this work is to take advantage of the serendipitous moments that arise naturally in our math classes. Remember, there is structure in much of the mathematical work our students do, and at any given point we have opportunities to help them be aware of it. Think of how often your students notice some regularity in mathematics that can be extended, applied to new situations, and/or generalized.

As students play around with the patterns or regularities, they usually begin to make claims about them. This provides a perfect launching point from which to explore structure. See, for example, the first-grade class below doing a *Number of the Day* activity during morning meeting. Their teacher, Ms. Ortiz, wrote the number *18* on the chart paper and asked students to create expressions that totaled that number. After a few examples were given, Alma suggested 18 + 32 − 32.

Teacher: How many of you think this equals 18? (A little more than half the hands go up.) Alma, can you explain how you know this works?

Alma: I know if you add something and then take it away, it's like it never happened.

Teacher: Did you add 18 and 32?

Alma: Not really. I don't even know what that is.

Teacher: You just knew if you added something to 18 and then took it away, it would still equal 18? (Alma nods and smiles.) You don't have to know what 18 plus 32 is?

Alma: Nope!

Teacher: That's an interesting strategy. I wonder if that works for other numbers. Maybe we can look for other examples where that happens.

Alma: I know it works. I just know it.

The next student who shared had another way to make 18, an idea unrelated to Alma's idea. And from there the class continued to share other ways to make 18. But Alma's sharing focused on some structures related to addition and subtraction. She noticed that when she added a certain quantity to a number and then removed what she had added, the result of the calculation was the original number. She felt confident enough in this idea to make an assertion that her strategy would work for other numbers. If Ms. Ortiz wanted to, she could put Alma's idea out to the class and challenge them to explore it to see if it works with other numbers. In doing so, her students would have an opportunity to notice and explore this structure. As they become confident with this idea, they may begin to make use of this structure in another context.

What's nice about the preceding exchange is that it illustrates how this early work with structure can be as simple as alerting students to the fact that ideas like these are worth paying attention to. Ms. Ortiz didn't make a huge lesson out of Alma's idea or require all students to stop what they were doing to explore other examples. Instead, she just invited students to look for other instances of this structure.

Teachers can also choose to take a deeper dive into this work with MP7 by choosing an idea and setting up a series of tasks or activities aimed at drawing students' attention to the structure(s) involved. One way to do this is by using students' conjectures about numbers, operations, shapes, measurement, and so forth as a launching point. By asking students to explore or even try to prove their conjectures with models or other representations, you are helping them understand the structure and be able to make use of it (Russell, Schifter, and Bastable 2011).

Following is a list of common claims that K–2 students might make at some point in their early math experiences. This list is by no means complete, but it can give you an idea of some topics you can explore with students when they come up in your classroom. I have categorized them, but I refrained from assigning particular grade levels because each class of students is unique and has different experiences, interests, and needs. Kids at any age may make one of these claims using their own phrasing and available vocabulary, but I wrote the claims in more adult-friendly language.

General Claims Primary Students Might Make in Math Class

Numbers

- Numbers have a set order.
- Our number system is organized by powers of ten (base ten).
  - If 10 is added to a two-digit number, the tens digit increases by 1.
  - Numbers can be added and subtracted by their place value.
- Even and Odd Numbers
  - Any number that can be broken into pairs without any left over can also be split into two equal teams without any left over.
  - Any number that has a leftover when broken into pairs will also have a leftover when it is split into two equal-size groups.
  - The sum of two even numbers is even.
  - The sum of two odd numbers is even.
  - The sum of an even and an odd number is odd.
  - Adding an even number of odd numbers results in an even answer.
  - Adding an odd number of odd numbers results in an odd answer.
  - Adding any number of even numbers results in an even answer.

Properties of Operations

- When you add any two numbers, you can reverse the order without changing the sum: $a + b = b + a$ (commutative).
- When adding three numbers, you can group them differently (while maintaining the same order) and the sum remains the same: $(a + b) + c = a + (b + c)$ (associative).
- Adding zero to any number results in a sum that is that number: $a + 0 = a$ (additive identity).

Other Behaviors of Operations

Addition

- Addition of positive numbers results in a sum larger than either addend.
- When you add 1 to an amount, the result is the next counting number.
  - $5 + 1 = 6$

- When you add an amount to an addend in an addition expression, the sum increases by that amount.
  - $4 + 5 = 9$ so $(4 + 1) + 5 = (9 + 1)$ or $5 + 5 = 10$
- When you subtract an amount from an addend in an addition expression, the sum decreases by that same amount.
  - $4 + 5 = 9$ so $(4–1) + 5 = (9–1)$ or $3 + 5 = 8$
- When you add an amount to an addend and subtract the same amount from the other addend, the sum remains the same.
- Start with two numbers where the first number is larger than the second number (for example, $8 > 5$). If you add the same number to each, the first total will be larger than the second total: $(8 + 2 > 5 + 2)$.

Subtraction

- The order of the numbers in a subtraction problem matters.
- When you subtract 1 from an amount, the result will be the previous counting number.
- You can decompose the subtrahend and subtract the parts from the minuend to get the difference of the original subtraction.
- If you add the same amount to both the minuend and the subtrahend, the difference will remain the same.
- If you subtract the same amount from both the minuend and the subtrahend, the difference will remain the same.
- Subtracting zero from a number results in a difference that is that number.
- If you subtract a number from itself, the result will be zero.

Relationship Between Addition and Subtraction

- If you add an amount to a quantity and then subtract that same amount, the result is your original quantity.
- Addition and subtraction have a part-part-whole relationship.
  - Part 1 + Part 2 = Whole $(a + b = c)$
  - Part 2 + Part 1 = Whole $(b + a = c)$
  - Whole – Part 1 = Part 2 $(c – a = b)$
  - Whole – Part 2 = Part 1 $(c – b = a)$
- You can solve a subtraction problem as a missing-addend problem.
- You can solve a missing-addend problem as a subtraction problem.

It's important to consider the needs and interests of the students in your class before deciding on a structure to explore with them. Some structures are more complex than others, and not every student will be ready to make generalizations about them.

My second graders, for example, were exploring what happens when operating with odd and even numbers. Early in our work, Jonathan said he noticed that adding an even number of odd numbers would give you an even answer. This was a powerful statement, and I was initially tempted to go down that path with the rest of the class. However, I noticed that most of my students were not 100 percent solid on why adding pairs of odd numbers and pairs of even numbers resulted in even answers but adding an odd and an even resulted in an odd answer. Sure, they could say odd + odd = even, but very few could really defend that statement with a representation, story context, or diagram. Their only arguments were that it worked with the examples they tried. For them, the fact that they tested the statement a bunch of times and it worked each time was good enough.

I decided not to explore Jonathan's conjecture with the whole class, but encouraged him to work on it with a few other classmates who I felt confident were ready to think about that idea. I chose to have the rest of the class continue to work on creating representations to prove odd + odd = even, even + even = even, and odd + even = odd. This decision allowed each student in class to work on an idea that was appropriate for him or her. In the end both groups shared their thinking and we worked to connect their ideas, making their work accessible to everyone.

Once you have selected an idea to explore with students, it is important to provide them with time and multiple opportunities to understand the structure involved. One effective way to do this is to ask students to prove or defend a general claim or conjecture by creating representations using manipulatives, diagrams, or story contexts (Russell et al. 2017). This work requires that students build an understanding of why a particular structure exists because they have to go beyond giving a few examples. When students can create representations that show why a particular idea always works, it is evidence that they have a solid understanding of some aspect of its structure. Consider the model in Figure 7.4 created on the Smartboard by one of my second graders, Olivia, to show why adding any two odd numbers results in an even answer.

Figure 7.4 Olivia's model

Olivia represented odd numbers as pairs of blue cube stacks with one odd yellow on top because she knew that even numbers can be grouped in pairs and odd numbers will have one left over. She showed the action of addition by having the stacks placed next to each other. She also covered the stacks to show that each blue pair could be any even number, because, in her words, "We don't know how many cubes are under the box." She concluded her representation by circling the two yellow cubes, showing that when the first pair of blue cube stacks with the one yellow cube are combined with the other pair of blue cube stacks and one yellow cube, the yellows make another pair and thus the sum is made up of pairs. This makes it an even number.

This work came after we had spent about ten minutes a day for two weeks at the end of morning meeting exploring the question, "What happens when you add two odd numbers?" The class began by combining specific groups of cubes and noticing that they kept making even numbers. (See Figure 7.5.)

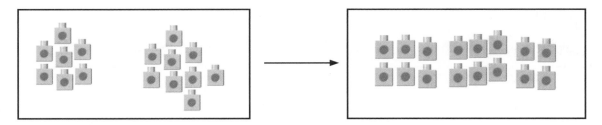

Figure 7.5 Grouping of cubes showing 7 + 9 = even

When I asked them to explore if it would always work, they tried bigger numbers and saw that they still got even numbers. (See Figure 7.6.)

When I asked if it would work with numbers so big we couldn't use cubes to make them, they said yes, but did not know how to show it. This brought us back to a discussion about what makes an odd number odd and an even number even. The groups explored this idea and eventually came up with two models: one showing pairs and one showing equal-size groups.

It was determined that we could show even numbers as pairs or two equal-size groups (Figure 7.7) and odd numbers by using the same representation but adding an extra cube (Figure 7.8). On the final day of our exploration, groups used these representations to show that an odd plus an odd equaled an even. The only problem was that their models didn't apply to all numbers, since the number of cubes was always finite. That's when Olivia suggested we cover our cube models with paper (or with a box on the Smartboard as seen in Figure 7.4).

This was powerful work, and I was very impressed with my second graders' thinking. Their representations unveiled a structure of our number system and

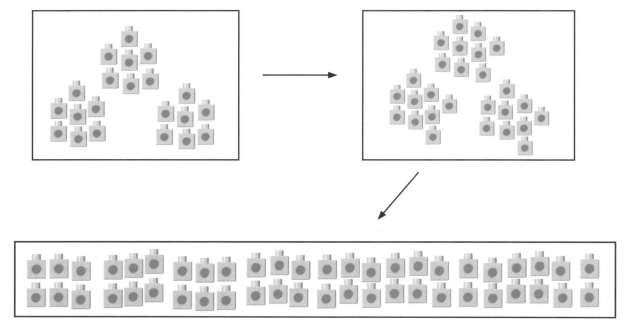

Figure 7.6 Grouping of cubes with a larger number of cubes showing 21 + 27 = even

gave them a deeper way in which to understand odd and even numbers.

If we want our students to build their understanding of structure, it is helpful to give them time to construct their knowledge through multiple experiences; our job is to facilitate the discussions, not tell them directly how to explore the ideas. I stayed out of my students' way. Instead of showing them the structures, I peppered

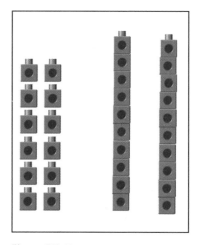

Figure 7.7 Even

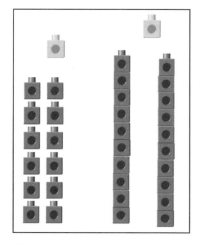

Figure 7.8 Odd

them with purposeful questions about their claims and representations to help draw their attention to important aspects about them.

As you guide students in this work, consider the kinds of questions you can ask them to push their thinking. What kind of open-ended questions would require them to consider the underlying structure behind their work? Questions such as *Why does this always work? How do you know that . . . ? What would happen if you . . . ?* help them make the connections and build understanding. You can also ask questions that have students describe the pattern they have noticed, such as *What are you noticing? You say that IT always works; what is the IT that always works?*

The following two vignettes provide other examples of teachers supporting MP7 with their students. As you read them, consider the role the teachers play and the kinds of questions they ask. How do their questions help kids focus on key ideas related to structure? What kinds of responses do their questions elicit? What other questions might you have asked if you were in these classrooms? Each vignette also has its own specific focus questions, but these global questions will help guide your thinking.

║ Focus Questions

1. When she introduces the first problem, Ms. Adams does not specify to which number they should add 1. What is the benefit of leaving the problem so open?
2. At one point, Ms. Adams is going to offer her idea about why Lizzy was getting confused, but changes her mind and asks if any students see what is tricky. How does this instructional strategy help all students in a discussion?
3. What role does the story context about gum play in the discussion? How does it help clarify the ideas students are discussing?
4. How does this lesson help students look for and make use of structure?

If You Have More Friends, You Have Less Gum

Ms. Adams—Grade 2, May

For the last three weeks, I have been working with my second graders to deepen their understanding of subtraction by exploring what happens when you change part of the problem. This work followed our recent work in addition exploring the results of changing the value of an addend. An outcome of the addition exploration was that my students made the conjecture "When you add an amount to one of the addends, the sum gets bigger by that same amount." This was powerful work. I wanted to see how they would think about subtraction and whether their claim applied to this operation, and if not, whether they could come up with a similar generalization that would work.

I knew this would be complicated, so I decided to start very small by asking them to consider what would happen when we added 1 to one of the numbers in a subtraction problem. I made their initial problem one that most of my second graders would not be able to solve right away. I wanted them to have to think about the way subtraction behaves without relying on calculating specific answers. I wrote $25 - 18 = 7$ and asked what would happen if we added 1 to either the 25 or the 18.

Charlie: The answer will go up by one.

Teacher: Can you tell us why?

Charlie: Because when we did this with addition, that's what happened.

Teacher: Can you be more specific? What happened?

Charlie: When we added 1 to one of the addends, the total went up by one.

Teacher: So you think the same thing will happen with subtraction? (He nods.) Who agrees with Charlie? (Half the students put their hands up.) What do others think?

Rose: I think it will go down by one, because subtraction is the opposite of addition, so you do the reverse. (Heads nod in agreement.)

Teacher: That's interesting. Who agrees with Rose? (About seven hands go up, two of them from people who originally agreed with Charlie.) I notice you all seem to be thinking really hard about this idea. Some think the answer will go up by one because that's what worked for addition, and some think the answer will go down by one because it's subtraction and you are thinking we should do the opposite.

At this point, I wanted to give them an opportunity to play around with these ideas but with smaller numbers so they could test their conjectures quickly without having to spend a lot of time performing calculations. I provided cubes, color tiles, graph paper, and colored pencils for students to use. I know most of my students would not need the manipulatives to solve the problems, but we have been working on using these tools as ways to show what is happening in the problems we explore. I wrote $9 - 6 =$ on the board and asked them to explore what happens when we add 1 to one of the numbers.

Students got right to work with their math partners. Some went to the cubes and tiles, and others used the graph paper and began drawing pictures. As I walked around, I checked in with students.

The first pair I joined was Brook and Gabby. They had stacks of cubes on their table and were feverishly making more stacks. I watched them work without saying anything. They were systematically making stacks and increasing the minuend each time. I was curious because I noticed they were representing the minuend and subtrahend as two separate stacks and placed them next to each other (Figure 7.9).

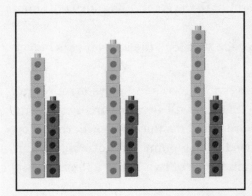

Figure 7.9 Brook and Gabby's cube stacks

I decided to check in to see what they were thinking about.

Teacher: What do you have going on here?
Gabby: We're making the first number go up and keeping the other number the same.
Teacher: And what are you discovering?
Gabby: I don't know yet (chuckles).
Brook: The answer gets bigger by one each time.
Teacher: Tell me more about that idea. Why does that happen?
Gabby: Ohhhh, I get it. We're making the first stack bigger by one so the answer gets bigger by one.

Teacher: Why do you think that is?
Brook: Because we're adding 1 each time.
Teacher: I see that, and that shows me how the 9 keeps getting bigger, but where is your answer in your model?
Gabby: Um . . .

Gabby was having trouble seeing it. She was used to the take-away representation with the cubes and not the comparison, but I thought it was good that she was working with Brook with this idea. I was sure it would help her see subtraction as comparison instead of just take-away. I decided to let Brook try to explain the representation to both help Gabby make sense of it and to help me get a sense of her thinking.

Teacher: Brook, can you tell us where the answer is in your representation?
Brook: It's the space between the stacks. See the first one? They match up at the 6 (points to the blue stack). The yellow is three higher so the answer is 3. And in the

next one the yellow is one higher, but we didn't change the blue, so the answer is one higher. It keeps happening.

Teacher: You think this will always happen?

Brook: Yeah. I guess so. I don't know, though.

Teacher: What makes you think it will always happen?

Brook: Well, you're just making the first stack bigger. Here's the answer. (She points to the space between the top of the blue stack and the top of the yellow stack.) When the first stack gets bigger, the answer gets bigger by the same amount. See . . . (She takes another yellow cube and adds it to the stack.) The answer is now one bigger.

Gabby: And if we add two yellows (takes two yellow cubes), the answer gets bigger by two.

This was huge! Gabby was not only connecting with Brook's comparison representation but also building on Brook's conjecture that this will always work by showing that when you increase the first number by more than one, the answer increases by that same amount. She hadn't totally generalized to that point, but noticing that an increase of two in the minuend resulted in an increase of two in the difference is a big idea.

I moved on to another group that was doing something different. Marty and Sean were using cubes, but unlike Gabby and Brook, they were using a removal model of subtraction. However, they were adding 1 to the subtrahend instead of the minuend like Gabby and Brook.

Teacher: What are you boys up to?

Marty: We saw a pattern. The answer keeps getting smaller by one.

Sean: See? (He indicates a pile of cubes.)

Teacher: Why do you think that's happening?

Sean: Because you keep taking more away, so it's getting smaller.

Teacher: What's getting smaller?

Sean: The pile left over. For 9 minus 6 you have 3 left. For 9 minus 7 you have 2 left. And for 9 minus 8 you just have 1 left.

Marty: Every time you take away m*ore, you make your leftover pile smaller.*

These two interactions capture the different kinds of thinking in the classroom. Some students used the difference model of subtraction, and others used removal. Some noticed that if you add to the minuend, the difference increases, and others noticed that if you increase the subtrahend, the difference got smaller. I was hoping to see these different ideas surface because it would make for a better discussion at the end.

I called the whole class together on the rug to try to pull the ideas together. I began by having Brook and Gabby share what they discovered and then had Sean and Marty share their ideas. We recorded their ideas on the Smartboard so the students could compare the ideas (see Figures 7.10 and 7.11).

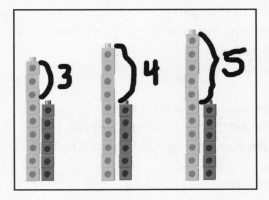

Figure 7.10 Brook and Gabby's representation

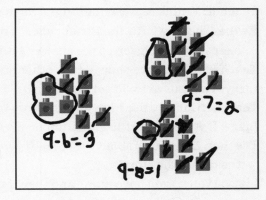

Figure 7.11 Sean and Marty's representation

Teacher: Some of you said adding 1 to a number in a subtraction problem would make the answer go up by one, and others said it would make the answer go down by one. We have two examples up on the board that prove each of those statements. How can that be?

Keisha: It depends on which number you add to. If you add to the first number, the answer gets bigger, and if you add to the second, the answer gets smaller. (Several heads are nodding in agreement.)

Teacher: But in addition we could add 1 to either of the numbers and the change would be the same. What's different here? (This is met with a pause as students think about it.)

Marty: I think it's 'cause the first number is what you have and the second number is your take-away.

Teacher: Can you say more about that?

Marty: It's, um . . . It's like if you have . . . gum and you give some to your friends. If you have more friends, you have less gum.

Teacher: Let's think about this, class, because I think Marty's idea about gum can help us think about what's happening here. Can someone else tell us what Marty is saying in their own words?

Brook: He's saying that if you have eight pieces of gum and you give a piece to all your friends, the more people there are, the more gum you have to share.

Teacher: And what does that do to the gum you have left?

Brook: You get less because you had to give more away.

Teacher: Which representation shows this gum example?

Kevin: The one with the green cubes. The second number is the take-away and it keeps getting bigger, so the answer gets smaller.

Teacher: What if we changed the other number?

Lizzy: Your answer will get bigger.

Teacher: Can you use Marty's gum story to explain why that happens?

Lizzy: If you add 1 to the first number, it's like putting more gum in the pack. Right?

Teacher: Let's think about the story. If you put more in the pack, how does that affect the rest of the story?

Lizzy: Well . . . you have more, and then if more friends come along . . . I'm confused.

Teacher: It can be confusing, but you're on to something. I think what's confusing is . . . (I hesitate here because I am about to point something out to her, but think maybe someone else could catch it instead.) Actually, does anyone see what's making this part tricky?

Sean: I think Lizzy was trying to change both numbers. She was adding gum to the pack and adding friends. You're supposed to just add gum for this one.

Teacher: What do you think, Lizzy?

Lizzy: Hmm . . . yeah, I think I got it. If you add 1 to the first number, you are putting more gum in the pack. And you just give the same number away so you get more at the end.

Teacher: Can anyone say it another way?

Gabby: It's basically like if you give more, you get less, and if you have more, you . . . get more? That doesn't make sense.

Teacher: Sure it does. Someone add to this.

Brook: If you take away more, you end up with less in the end, and if you give yourself more but take away the same, you end up with more.

Teacher: You are all doing some amazing thinking today. I'm wondering if we can state a rule about this work with subtraction like we did for addition. With addition you said that if you add 1 to an addend, the sum will increase by one. What would be the rule or rules for subtraction? Talk with your thinking buddy and then we'll report. (Kids talk for a bit, but I hurry this part along because it's almost time for recess.) Who can state a rule?

Keisha: If you add 1 to the first number in a subtraction problem, your answer goes up by one, and if you add 1 to the second number, the answer goes down by one.

Jordan: I think if you change it by any amount, the answer is going to change by that amount. Like if you add 5 to the first number, the answer is going to change by five.

Teacher: That's a big idea to think about, Jordan. Maybe we can explore that idea tomorrow. Right now we're out of time. But *you all worked really hard today. Nice job!*

We moved through this work much faster today than when we worked with addition. That surprised me, because subtraction is so much harder. I think it was because of the familiarity with this kind of work. It gets easier over time. We got to a great point today with the different rules for subtraction. Next time we are going to test those rules to see if they work. I can't wait to dive into this work again.

In this vignette Ms. Adams pushed students to think hard about some complicated mathematics. The task she had the class engage in shows the power of using representations to uncover structures.

Ms. Adams's choice to leave the task open about whether students added 1 to the minuend or subtrahend was very effective. It allowed the students to discover that there was a difference in how this operation behaved compared with their work with addition. She could have easily pointed out that it makes a difference which number gets changed, but that would have robbed students of the opportunity to see it for themselves. It added extra time to the lesson, but it was time well spent.

Ms. Adams's restraint in not pointing out Lizzy's confusion and instead throwing it back on the students was also very beneficial. Her choice made the kids think carefully about what was happening with Lizzy's work. Lizzy was trying to use a story context to explain the results in changing the minuend, but in her efforts she also began changing the subtrahend. Rather than fix her mistake, Ms. Adams left it to the class to explain it. The students, not Ms. Adams, had to identify what was right and what was confusing in Lizzy's idea, and they worked to clarify it, thereby strengthening their understanding. This is also an example of MP3: critique the reasoning of others.

Much of the students' class time was spent making representations with their partners. Some used cubes; others used number lines or made pictures. Physical and visual representations of mathematical ideas help students see structure and understand how a particular idea is constructed.

During the discussion, Marty used a story context of sharing gum. Ms. Adams took advantage of that moment by asking students to connect their thinking and representations about subtraction to a real-life context. That helped make this abstract concept meaningful and allowed students to see the idea from another angle. Using story contexts is a powerful way for students to represent their understanding of structure (Bastable 2012).

This lesson pushed students to consider how subtraction differs from addition and gave them opportunities to see how the operation behaved under certain circumstances. Ms. Adams will continue this kind of exploration as students work to refine their assertions and test them with other numbers. The investigation will eventually lead to general rules about subtraction that her students will apply in their daily work.

Not all work with structure, however, needs to be so involved, as shown by my second graders and with Ms. Adams's class. Primary teachers can draw students' attention to structure in more subtle ways, as seen in the next example with Ms. Rodriguez helping her kindergartners to see some structure in addition as they play a classroom game. As you read, consider the following questions.

Focus Questions

1. How are these kindergartners looking for and making use of structure?
2. How is the teacher supporting this work?
3. What's different about this work compared with that of the second graders in Ms. Adams's class?

We Don't Even Need to Add Them

Mrs. Rodriguez—Kindergarten, April

In the spring, my kindergartners were playing a game called *Compare* from the Investigations math curriculum. In this game, players each flip over a number card from their deck and compare the quantities, and the student with the larger quantity keeps the two cards. In our previous math lesson I introduced a new version of the game called *Double Compare*. In this version each player flips over two cards and compares the total amount of their cards to the total amount of their partner's cards. The student with the higher total keeps all the cards. My class loved this version, but some were clearly much faster at comparing totals than others.

For this particular lesson, I was interested in having the students focus on the various strategies they used to compare the totals. I decided to start the lesson by having students play the game in pairs so I could circulate and get a sense of how different students were playing the game. The first pair I came to was Zoe and Chen, who had the cards in Figure 7.12 showing.

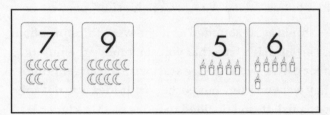

Figure 7.12 Zoe's cards (left) and Chen's (right) in a game of *Compare*

Zoe used her fingers and counted aloud, "Ten, 11, 12, 13, 14, 15, 16" while Chen said "Six" aloud and then pointed to the pictures of candles on the 5 card and counted up, "Seven, 8, 9, 10, 11." I decided to hear from them so I could find out what they were thinking.

Teacher: I noticed you each counted on to find your total. I'm wondering why you each started by putting the second number in your head and counted on from there.

Zoe: It's easier.

Teacher: Why?

Zoe: 'Cause you don't have to count as much.

Teacher: That's interesting. What about you, Chen?

Chen: Yeah, it's like this, you see (points to the cards). Six is bigger than five. So you just count this (holds up five fingers) instead of this (holds up six fingers).

Teacher: I know when we practice reading we start on this side, the left, and go this way, to the right. (I pointed to the left and moved my hand to the right.) We don't have to start with the number that is on the left side?

Chen: Nope. It's the same no matter what. (He takes the 6 and 5 cards and switches them around a bunch of times.)

Zoe: You can't always do it. Just in this game.

Teacher: Sometimes you have to go in that order from left to right?

Zoe: Yeah, like when it's on paper.

Teacher: What do you mean?

Zoe: When you give us a paper to do and it has like 3 plus 4 on it, we have to start with the 3.

Teacher: But with the cards it doesn't matter?

Zoe: Uh-huh. Because you can move them like this. (She switches her cards.)

Teacher: So if you can move them with your hands, then you can switch the order, but if it's on paper, you have to add it in the order in which it's written?

Zoe: Yep.

Teacher: That's an interesting idea, Zoe. We'll have to think about that some more to see if it's true. Maybe I can add it to our "Ideas We Are Considering" poster.

It was interesting to hear Zoe's thinking. It sounded as if she were thinking about physically switching the numbers around. It's true that you can't move the numbers on a sheet, but you can move number cards. I've seen Zoe start with the larger number and count on regardless of how they were written, but perhaps this idea was not solid with her yet. I knew I didn't have to push it, so I decided to move on. My kindergartners come up with some crazy ideas sometimes and I don't want to squash them, so I just make a point of saying something that validates their thinking but doesn't make them think their idea is totally right. I made a note about this exchange so I would know to return to it at some point before moving on. By the end of the year, I want Zoe and Chen to realize that, in any context, you can reverse the order of addends and the sum will remain the same.

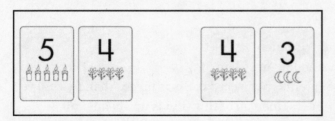

Figure 7.13 Zuseth's cards (left) and Javionna's (right) in a game of *Double Compare*

The next pair I came upon was Zuseth and Javionna. They had made an interesting discovery that they were excited to share. Figure 7.13 depicts the cards that were showing when I joined them.

Zuseth: Ms. Rodriguez, look at this. We don't even have to count them.

Teacher: What do you mean?

Zuseth: We only have to look at these (points to the 5 and 3).

Teacher: Why can you do that?

Javionna: The fours are the same.

Zuseth: These (holds the fours up) match. But Javionna only has a 3 and I have a 5.

Teacher: You know you have more without even adding them?

Zuseth: Uh-huh. We never have to add them.

Teacher: So this worked on other turns? (They both nod.)

I looked at their recording sheet and sure enough, in every turn they each had one number that was the same. I decided to watch them play a while longer to see what they would do when they got a set when that didn't happen. I didn't have to wait long. On the next turn they flipped over the cards in Figure 7.14.

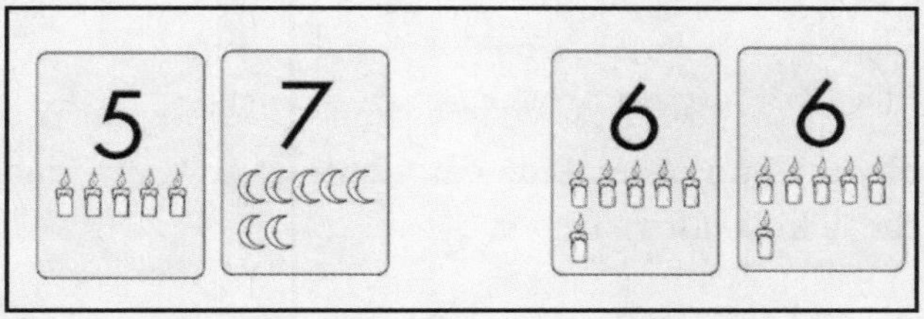

Javionna: Aw, man.

Teacher: What?

Javionna: I have to count them.

Teacher: Why?

Javionna: 'Cause we don't have any matches.

Teacher: So you need matches for your idea to work?

Figure 7.14 Zuseth's cards (left) and Javionna's (right)

Zuseth: Yeah. It only works with matches.

Teacher: Why do you think that is?

Zuseth: (Shrugs.) If they match, you just look at the other numbers.

Teacher: Why don't you have to think about the other numbers?

Javionna: They're the same.

Teacher: Can you show me with cubes why that works? What if you each had a 2, but Javionna had a 4 and Zuseth had 5?

Zuseth: I have more.

Teacher: Can you show me with cubes why that idea of matches works?

They each get cubes to match the cards I said they had. Meanwhile I got the actual cards out so we could match the cubes to their cards. It looked like Figure 7.15.

Teacher: Explain how this idea works.

Zuseth: See these twos? (She points to both stacks of two cubes.) They are the same so you can just cover them.

Teacher: I guess I'm wondering why you can just forget about them.

Javionna: If we just had two each, we're tied. Then she gets a 5 and I get a 4, so she beats me.

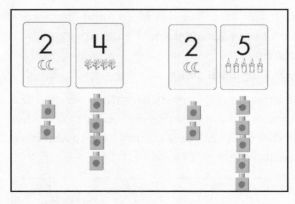

Figure 7.15 Cards with matching cube amounts

Teacher: That's an interesting strategy. So if you have the same cards, it's like you're tied and the other card tells you who wins?
Javionna: Yeah.

My kindergartners never cease to amaze me. Sometimes their thinking is hard to articulate at first, but when we play around with manipulatives or talk it out together, their thinking gets clearer and other kids can connect to their ideas. It's always an adventure with these kids. I love it.

In these examples, young students worked on the ideas of MP7. We saw the first group exploring whether you can switch the order of the numbers when adding. The second group began to generalize a rule that always seemed to work when comparing sums of two addends.

None of the students was anywhere close to coming up with formal explanations of the structures they were exploring, but that is not expected of K–2 students. It is enough for them to be noticing these ideas and exploring them over time with the support of their teacher. Primary teachers lay an important mathematical foundation for students by engaging them in this kind of thinking early on, and these kinds of habits of mind will help them throughout their entire mathematical career.

Ms. Rodriguez saw some interesting thinking related to MP7 and decided to press on those ideas in the moment. Her questions had a few purposes. First, they alerted students to the notion that there was something compelling about their discoveries. Her questions also prompted her students to think more deeply about what they noticed so they could begin trying to articulate some of the ideas. Ms. Rodriguez was also able to get a stronger sense of where her students were with these ideas and where they might go next. After these brief exchanges, she left her students to continue their work. This was a good example of how teachers can support MP7 without creating a long series of explorations.

This work is not easy, particularly if these ideas are new to us. Teachers can benefit from professional learning opportunities that help develop their own conceptual understanding of mathematics. I found that when I worked on projects with other teachers around developing algebraic reasoning in primary and elementary grades, I became much better at recognizing when students were encountering ideas related to MP7. Another possibility is to create a book study group within your own grade or school that features a text you explore together. I highly recommend *Connecting Arithmetic to Algebra* (2011) by Susan Jo Russell, Deborah Schifter, and Virginia Bastable. This book and related coursework formed the basis for my work around MP7 in my own classroom.

Young children quite often make use of structures before they have the ability to articulate what they are doing. In fact, sometimes you will see your students applying an idea connected with structure and can use it as your launching point for this kind of work.

When you engage students in this work with MP7, you are empowering them by giving them a greater understanding of our number system, operations, geometry, or any other mathematical ideas they encounter. As students deepen their knowledge of structures by creating representations, making models, or using story contexts, they will begin to see ways in which they can apply this thinking in other situations. Like Keisha and her approach to subtraction, when students understand how a particular mathematical idea is constructed, they can use it to their advantage. It's our job to provide students with the opportunities, time, and guidance to help them explore and understand the structure of mathematics.

CHAPTER 8

Mathematical Practice 8: Look For and Express Regularity in Repeated Reasoning

hen my family and I were planning and preparing to drive from Massachusetts to North Carolina for our vacation, we talked a lot about ways the kids could entertain themselves in the car. The kids suggested travel games, books, music, and all sorts of other activities to occupy themselves on our 16-hour road trip. Then my 11-year-old daughter suggested that we sing "100 Bottles of Beer on the Wall" . . . the whole way. We laughed, but then she started working it out.

First, she timed herself singing the first verse and discovered it took 9 seconds. Next, she she multiplied that by 100 to figure out how long it would take to sing the whole song, and got 900 seconds. She wanted to work in minutes, so she divided 900 by 60 and announced that it would take 15 minutes to sing the whole song. She paused for a moment while she thought and then said, "We need to start with a lot more bottles of beer."

At this point she started adding up the times. She said, "100 bottles takes 15 minutes so 200 bottles takes 30 minutes and 300 bottles takes 45 minutes, 400 bottles takes an hour, 500 bottles will take an hour and fifteen minutes."

She continued with this repeated reasoning until she got to 800 bottles taking two hours. Then she paused for a moment before grabbing her phone to use the calculator. After a quick calculation, she proudly announced, "So we're going to need to start with 6,400 bottles of beer if we're going to sing the whole way to North Carolina!"

After an intial shudder at the thought of hearing that song for 16 hours, I had a proud dad moment. I was impressed by her reasoning and also curious about how she went from calculating in 15-minute chunks to what appeared to be a formula. I asked her to explain what she did. She said, "I kept adding 100 bottles at a time and it was taking forever. I noticed when I got to 800 that it was two hours, and I realized every hour is 400 bottles. So all we have to do is multiply however many hours our trip is by 400 and that will tell us how many bottles we need to start with."

Alli was repeating the same calculation and reasoning as she added a series of 100 bottles of beer. Once she got to 800 bottles she noticed that every 400 bottles took one hour to sing. Her repeated reasoning helped her to see some regularity in her work. She was then able to create a shorter method for solving the problem. She expressed this regularity when she said, "I realized every hour is 400 bottles."

This example captures the essense of what it means to look for and express regularity in repeated reasoning. Alli's repeated calculation helped her to see some regularity that she could then use to create a more efficient and generalizable strategy. It's not a perfect formula, because it doesn't account for extra time to sing numbers with lots of syllables (e.g., six-thousand, seven-hundred, and seventy-seven bottles of beer on the wall), but it did give us a good ballpark figure from which to start. Thankfully though, the kids abandoned the song before we even made it to the highway.

In my experience, looking for and talking about regularity is something primary-grade students absolutely love to do. No matter what grades or classes I visit, I always run into situations where students comment about some pattern they've noticed. It makes sense when you think about the excitement that comes from discovering some regularity in mathematics. It's as if they've uncovered some secret, hidden idea and unlocked its potential. Time and time again, I listen to kids say things such as "That's so cool!" or "Whoa!" when they discover regularity.

Mathematical Practice 8 for primary students is all about this work with regularity; the mathematical world is full of regularities just waiting to be discovered. Students experience the idea of regularity by first looking for things that happen consistently as they repeatedly reason through a series of related problems. For example, after trying many examples of adding one to different numbers, kindergartners might notice that the result is the next counting number. Their repeated reasoning helped them see that the same thing keeps happening. First graders might notice that when using pattern blocks, 2 trapezoids make 1 hexagon, 4 trapezoids make 2 hexagons, 6 trapezoids make 3 hexagons, and so on. In both cases, the regularity presents itself naturally in the tasks students are doing through their repeated reasoning.

The second part of MP8 is about expressing regularity. This basically means that after students identify something that seems to happen consistently (for example, adding one results in the next counting number), they describe it to others. This description is typically a kind of conjecture, something the student believes to be true but has yet been proven. For example, a kindergartner might say, "When I add one, I get the next number." In doing so, the student is expressing the regularity in a general sense. He isn't talking about a single instance like 5 + 1, but making a bigger conceptual leap—that adding one gets you the next number.

Consider another example from a first-grade classroom. When working on addition and subtraction, a few students noticed that after adding two numbers (3 + 2 = 5), taking away the amount they added resulted in the starting number (5 – 2 = 3). Their teacher decided to capitalize on this and ask them if it would work with other numbers to encourage them to try more examples. As they explored other examples such as 4 + 1 = 5, so 5–1 = 4 and 6 + 3 = 9, so 9 – 3 = 6, the students strengthened their understanding of this regularity and began to express it in the form of a conjecture or rule. In the words of one student, "When you add something and then take it away, it's like you did nothing." In other words, if you add an amount to a number and then subtract that same amount, your result is the original number.

MP8, Look For and Express Regularity in Repeated Reasoning, like MP7, Look For and Make Use of Structure, requires intentionality on the part of the teacher to make the ideas explicit. In the above examples about related facts, the students could have just encountered the pattern they saw with the equations and moved on with their math work without giving the regularity much thought. But when their teachers pushed on the ideas, the regularities took on a deeper level of importance and the students were able to capitalize on them. Think of the benefit to the other kindergartners when the small group shared their thinking about how adding one to a number always gets you the next number. The next time these students are presented with problems that involve adding one, it is likely that some will recognize that the answer is the next counting number based on the work around this regularity.

As students recognize regularities in their mathematical world through solving a series of related problems, they begin to develop strategies and shortcuts that make use of these regularities. That's the point of having students engage in this kind of work. We want our students to develop efficient strategies and to have meaningful shortcuts that make sense to them. Consider what the following second graders did when working on a set of near-double addition facts and how their teacher worked to support them in this endeavor. It was her hope that some, if not all, students would notice some regularity in this work.

Teacher: Tell me what you noticed.

Sam: Well . . . we did this (shows his paper with the following):

$$7 + 7 = 14$$
$$7 + 6 = 13$$
$$6 + 6 = 12$$
$$6 + 5 = 11$$
$$5 + 5 = 10$$
$$5 + 4 = 9$$

Teacher: Interesting. Can you tell me what you discovered?

Jesse: We discovered that when you have two numbers next to each other, you can just think of the double and the answer is one less.

Teacher: What do you mean when you say two numbers next to each other?

Sam: Like 5 and 6 or 3 and 4.

Jesse: Yeah, if you're adding numbers that are one away from each other. You can use the double.

Teacher: Tell me more about what "using the double" means.

Jesse: It's like this. See? (Points to the 7 + 6.) You might not know 7 + 6, but if you do 7 + 7 'cause it's easy, then you just take away 1 from 14 and get 13.

Teacher: And that always works?

Jesse: Yep. It worked for all of these that we tried.

Teacher: Could you state it as a rule? Like what if you were going to tell me the rule for solving addition problems with numbers that are one away from each other?

Jesse: Hmm . . . I guess something like when you have to add numbers that are next to each other and you don't know what it is, you just have to double one number and get the answer. Then take away 1 to get your other answer.

Sam: Yeah, these are like almost doubles. So you just have to think of the double that they can be and go from there.

Teacher: I like that phrase, *almost doubles*. So the rule for solving an almost double is to solve the double that it's close to and then subtract 1?

Sam: Or add 1 if you use the smaller double.

Teacher: Interesting. So you can double either the bigger number or the smaller number?

Sam: Yeah. It doesn't matter.

Teacher: Help me finish this rule. When solving almost doubles . . .

Sam: You solve the double it's close to. If you do the bigger number, you take away 1, and if you do the smaller number, you add 1.

Teacher: Could you use this strategy for every almost double and have it will work? (Both nod their heads.) How about with bigger numbers like 11 plus 12?

Jesse: Easy! Eleven and 11 is 22, so one less . . . I mean, one more is 23.

These second graders began by exploring some near-doubles facts with the rest of the class. As they worked, they noticed that each near double was just one away from a double fact they already knew. As they worked with the teacher to articulate this claim, they began to solidify what would become a powerful addition strategy for problems of this type. The teacher supported the students and kept the ownership of the articulation with them. She worked to help them clarify their assertions.

K–2 teachers support their students in this practice standard by paying close attention to when these opportunities naturally arise or by providing students with tasks that help make a particular regularity explicit. In the near-doubles example, the teacher deliberately gave students this set of problems in the hope that they might notice that every near double is one away from a double. Her intention was to have students "discover" this regularity so the ideas would come from them rather than from her. Conversely, in the previous first-grade example, two students stumbled upon the idea that when you add an amount and take it away, your starting amount remains. This was not part of the teacher's math session, but she decided to take advantage of the moment when it came up.

The key to engaging students in MP8 is to stimulate their general interest in what a particular regularity is and why it exists. One effective strategy is to be curious about these ideas yourself. Students love to feel like you're puzzling through an idea with them, and get excited when they feel like they are teaching you. By suspending what you already know and understand about our number system, operations, geometry, and so on, you open the learning up for students to discover the ideas themselves. Rather than explain why a particular regularity exists, ask questions of the students instead. The following are some examples of effective questions:

- What do you see happening?
- Will that always work?
- What would happen if . . . ?
- How do you know?
- Can you create a rule for . . . ?
- If a visitor came to our class and they didn't know what you had discovered, what could you say so they would understand your idea?

Each question requires students to do the investigating and articulating. The last example is particularly helpful with young students. Kids love the idea of an outside guest popping in so they have opportunities to share their discoveries. I would take this a step further and actually ask other teachers and even the principal to visit our classroom on occasion so the kids could enlighten them. The point is that when we take a backseat and allow our students to discover regularities, develop their understanding of them, and then support them as they begin to express these regularities in the form of general claims or conjectures, we are effectively working on MP8.

The following vignettes explore MP8 further. Here students begin by reviewing some work they did exploring the commutative property. The teacher then had them explore what happens when you remove one from one addend and add it to the other addend. As you read, it's helpful to pay attention to the roles the students and teachers play. The questions the teachers ask are particularly useful to note.

|| Focus Questions

1. What prior learning experiences does Ms. Solomon provide to prepare students for this work?
2. How does her three-step process support the learning?
3. In this vignette, we can see a lot of the reflection and intentionality as the session unfolds. What does that say about the nature of this work?

It's the Circle of Life!

Ms. Solomon—Grade 1, June

I started the year wondering how far one could take a group of first graders in noticing and expressing regularity. I had done some of this work in a multiage class with both first and second graders, but what could a group of first graders do on their own? I knew my first graders were good at noticing regularity, but could they actually express it in the form of a conjecture or generalization?

To help them, I created a three-step process that could help guide their thinking and posted it on the chart paper. I explained that in math, we often see patterns or things that happen over and over and that it's important for us to think about why that happens. I then told them they would go through the following steps as we considered a pattern we have talked about a lot this year with addition.

1. Notice something.
2. Show it with cubes.
3. Make a rule.

I decided I would start this discussion by having them generate the list of ways to make ten with two addends. When we got to 5 + 5, I reminded them that when I'd gotten to this point in a previous discussion of this list, they had told me something about 6 + 4 and 4 + 6. That's when Rachel chimed in, "They're exactly the same thing except the other way around."

Teacher: Does that always work?

Students: Yes!

Teacher: This seems like a good place to try out our steps. You all seem to have noticed that you can switch them and get the same answer. Let's try Step 2.

The students worked to make stacks of four and six and then began switching them back and forth to model the action of reversing the addends. This seemed like an easy exercise for them, so I decided to move them on to Step 3.

Teacher: Does anyone think they have a rule they can say for what's happening?

Chris: When you switch the numbers, you still have the same total cubes.

Teacher: When you say switch the numbers, are you talking about the addends?

Chris: Yes, when you switch the addends, you keep the same total. It doesn't change.

Teacher: So our rule can be that when we add, we can switch the addends and the total or sum will stay the same?

Class: Yes.

With that out of the way, the question remained whether we could talk about a more complicated regularity using the same steps. They knew the process; at least they had experienced the process, with an accessible piece of math. In the past, I hadn't been able to tell if it was the process that was hard or the math that was hard. Now I had seen that they could have success with the process in this context. Would the process stay accessible as the math got harder?

We began the next piece the following day by generating the whole list of ways to make ten using two addends. I decided that this time we would skip making the same observations we had made in the previous discussions with the hope that if we started further along the process, we could end further along the process.

Teacher: What do you notice when you look at this list?

Bailey: A number gets lower and a number gets higher.

Noah: One number goes down and the next goes up and the answer is still 10.

Teacher: We just noticed something. Can we show it with cubes?

Noah came up and got a train of ten cubes and began removing cubes one at a time. As he did this, I asked what number sentence each move showed to connect the representation with the numbers.

Teacher: What did Noah do to turn 10 + 0 into 9 + 1?

Sydney: One gets higher and one gets lower, so it's just taking one off the 9 and going to the 1. (She referred to making it into 8 + 2.)

Teacher: So you can take one off of this stack and put it over here? And then it's 8 plus 2?

Juliana: Seven plus 3.

Teacher: And then it's 7 plus 3.

Chelsea: Six plus 4.

Teacher: You all see that happening? (Heads nod.) So, if we did the first two parts, we noticed something, and we used Noah's way to show it with cubes. What's the next step?

Students: Make a rule.

Teacher: Can you help me write a rule that would tell other people what's happening here and how it works?

Students: Yeah!

Teacher: Yeah? How do you all think we should start? Do you want to talk to your neighbors first about the rule or do you want to just talk all together?

They chose all together, so I cautioned them that I needed to hear everybody participating and gave them a quiet minute to think first. Then we continued our whole-group conversation.

Emma: I have something I noticed.

Teacher: Okay, what did you notice?

Emma: That . . . Can I show it?

Teacher: Uh-huh . . . Can you use your words to tell it while you show it?

Emma: (Taking the train of ten cubes) When this goes off, it starts as 1 and this goes down from 10, 9, and then . . . (She looks for help from her friend.)

Chloe: Counting backward!

Emma: This goes 2 and this goes 8.

Noah: Exactly like that! (She points to the chart.)

Emma: It's 2 plus 8.

Teacher: Emma, hold on one second. Chloe, what are you noticing?

Chloe: That is exactly like those. (She points to the chart.)

Chloe was making a connection between what was written on the chart and the cube model that Emma was using, and was so excited, she was nearly jumping off the floor.

Teacher: What do you mean?

Chloe: It's like 10, 9, 8, 7, 6, 5, 4, 3, 2, 1, 0.

Teacher: Emma, is that what you were trying to say? That the cubes . . .

Emma: (Each time moving a cube to make the new pair of addends) Four plus 6 and then 5 plus 5 and then 6 plus 4 again and then 7 plus 3 again, and then you have 8 plus 2 instead of 2 plus 8, and then you've got 1 plus 9 and . . . And then it starts all over again. Zero plus 10.

Teacher: Zero plus 10, just like this one. Chloe, do you want to add something?

Chloe: I just wanted to say that one number's getting higher and one number's getting lower.

Ava: You keep taking them off until there's all 10 and there's like 0 over here.

Bailey: Like the circle of life! (Laughter.)

Teacher: That's funny! I want to start singing the "Lion King" now. (Laughter.) Okay, back to business. It kind of makes the same thing. Raise your hand if you have a picture in your head now that matches what's going on with the numbers. If you can imagine the cubes matching what's happening with these numbers, raise your hand. (Most hands go up.)

At this point I decided to prompt them further in terms of stating a rule by giving them a sentence frame. I wrote, *When you . . .* on chart paper and then asked if anybody would like to state a rule using this beginning.

Sydney: When you get a number . . . you just . . . When you get a number and you just turn it around. It's the same thing because it's the same numbers . . . like . . . yeah.

I wondered, did this have meaning in this context or was this just the other rule again? It sounded very much like the rule for the commutative property we explored earlier.

Teacher: Okay, so that sounds like this rule, the switching-around rule. Is that the same thing that is happening here when you were removing cubes?

Sydney: No . . . it's different.

Chloe: How about when you take one off the first train and put it on the second train, it doesn't change anything?

Teacher: That seems to describe what you were doing. I think I'll write this down and we can pick up here tomorrow.

As we head into the end of the year, I think that this work with looking for and expressing regularity is accessible to first graders. I think they can make the representations after being really familiar with the idea, having noticed it and used it many times. And I think that when it gets to the point that what is happening is taken for granted and is obvious to most of the class, as it was with the switch-around, they can even make a generalization. It is a long and slow process with first graders and takes a lot of visits to the same place. But it's worth the effort, because so much learning and deepening of understanding happens during the process.

Ms. Solomon's vignette demonstrates the complex nature of this work for young students. MP8 is not something that begins and ends in one simple session. These ideas need to be revisited in multiple ways, and students need to experience the mathematics enough so they are comfortable looking deeply into why certain regularities exist. Ms. Solomon intentionally spent time on these ideas over the course of the year to give her students opportunities to become comfortable with the mathematics. As a result, her students learned things such as the following: the order doesn't matter when you add; there is a set number of ways to make a particular sum with two addends; the pattern seems to repeat (the circle of life); and when you take one amount from one addend and add it to the other, the sum remains the same.

These are very important understandings that students need to support their development of mathematical reasoning skills. By taking the time to continually revisit this pattern and asking her students to consider what's happening and why, Ms. Solomon has engaged her students in the kind of thinking described in MP8. Not every student reached the same milestone in this session. It's important to note that these ideas develop on a continuum. Some students are at a point where they can begin to express the regularity in the form of a generalization, whereas others still need to model the ideas with cubes. But all students benefit from this kind of activity because there are multiple entry points for the range of learners. While some are considering why this regularity exists, others are getting opportunities to construct their understanding of combinations that total ten.

Having a chart with some basic steps students can take when doing this kind of thinking was helpful. They were able to see that if they noticed something through their repeated reasoning, they could demonstrate it with cubes to better understand what's happening and then come up with a rule that applies that understanding. I also think it was helpful that Ms. Solomon chose an idea they all felt comfortable with when she first introduced the chart. In this way students could work through the steps with a familiar concept to understand the process. It made the work with the more challenging mathematical ideas more accessible to them.

Now let's look at another classroom where students are working on looking for and expressing regularity in repeated reasoning. In this second-grade classroom, students are working on building towers that grow at a constant rate (three rooms per floor, six rooms per floor, and so on). Their teacher also has them recording their results on a table that will help highlight some key patterns. Just as with the previous vignette, pay close attention to the ways in which the teacher engages her students and how this work takes time.

‖ Focus Questions

1. What regularities are present in this task?
2. What would you want your students to pay attention to?
3. What was the benefit of having the students who doubled to solve for ten floors share last after others who used less efficient approaches?

It's the Doubling Rule!
Ms. Chan—Grade 2, March

My second graders were beginning work on patterns and repeated addition during the same time we were studying fairy tales. I decided to combine the two in a math activity called *Constructing Castle Towers*. This activity was adapted from a unit in *Investigations in Number, Data, and Space* called *Cube Buildings* (TERC 2016). We used snap cubes for this activity, and I explained that each cube represented a room within the tower and a row of cubes represented one floor of the tower. Therefore, a tower that had two cubes on the bottom with two cubes stacked on top would be a two-story tower with four rooms (see Figure 8.1).

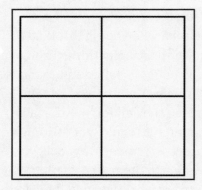

Figure 8.1 Tower example

Their task was to create towers with the same number of rooms on each floor and then determine the total number of rooms for a given number of floors. They would record this information on a table that looked like Figure 8.2.

I began by showing students a three-floor tower with two rooms on each floor (Figure 8.3) to help them understand what cubes represent in this task.

I then asked questions such as *How many rooms are in each floor of my tower? How many floors do I have? How many rooms altogether? What if I built this tower higher? How many rooms would there be if the tower had five floors? Eight floors? How do you know?* As students answered these questions, I filled in the corresponding information on the table. After some restating and modeling by students who understood the idea, most seemed comfortable with the terms and rules. I then sent them to their seats and showed them a floor of a tower made with three cubes in an L shape (see Figure 8.4).

They had to make this shape with cubes and then make another floor on top of it. Once they demonstrated this understanding, I gave them the next directions, which were to make the L-shaped tower five stories high and then predict how many rooms there would be if their tower were ten stories. This was a tall order, but I was confident they could do this.

Total Number of Floors in the Tower	Total Number of Rooms in the Tower
1	3
2	6
3	9
4	12

Figure 8.2 Tower table

Students worked for a while on the task and had a variety of approaches. Once everyone was finished, I called the class to the floor to discuss their strategies for figuring the total number of rooms for ten floors.

Teacher: You all built the same tower. You started with 3 rooms on the first floor and had to build up to 10 floors. What I want to know is what was happening as your towers grew.

Lori: You're adding a new floor.

Kevin: It started wobbling and it wouldn't stay up good.

Teacher: What else happened as you kept adding floors?

Stacy: It goes up three each time.

Teacher: Lori said that your towers kept getting a new floor. Stacy said that each time you made a new floor, it went up three. And Kevin said that when your tower got high, it started to wobble. Anything else?

(No response.)

Teacher: Okay, now I want you to share how you figured out how many rooms there would be when your towers had 10 floors. How did you figure it out?

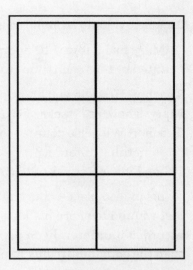

Figure 8.3 Three-floor tower with two rooms on each floor

Lori: First I went up to … um … 5 rooms. Then I went … I mean, 5 floors. First I went up to 5 floors and I knew there were 15 rooms. Then I counted up from there.

Teacher: Can you show us how you counted?

Lori put her finger on the fifth row and said 15. Then she put her finger on the sixth row and counted by ones (16, 17, 18). She did this all the way up the tower. It was an interesting way to keep track. However, I was surprised she chose to count on. Lori is very strong mathematically. I had assumed she would double her total for 5 floors.

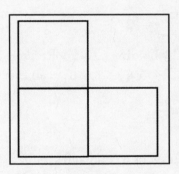

Figure 8.4 L-shaped tower footprint

Teacher: Who used a strategy similar to Lori's? Well, first, what strategy did Lori use?

Mitch: She counted.

Teacher: Did she count all the cubes or count on from 15?

Mitch: She counted on from 15.

Teacher: Okay, so who else used a counting-on strategy? (Three hands go in the air.) Who tried something different?

Mary: I counted by tens.

Teacher: Could you come up and show us?

Mary had a tower 10 floors high. She drew her finger up the three columns and counted by tens each time (10, 20, 30).

Teacher: How did you know you could count this by tens?

Mary: These are stacks of 10 (pointing to the columns).

Teacher: Who else counted by tens to figure this out? (Two hands go up.) Who tried something different?

Brian: I made 3 sticks of 10 (holds up his paper). And the answer is 30.

Brian also used a counting-by-tens strategy, but either he didn't realize it or he just wanted to share his idea. Although his idea was almost identical to Mary's, he recorded it differently on paper. He actually showed the three "sticks" of 10 rather than the equation 10 plus 10 plus 10 like Mary did.

Teacher: Do you think your strategy might be a counting-by-tens strategy?

Brian: Yeah, it is.

Teacher: How?

Brian: I have 3 tens. So it goes 10, 20, 30.

Teacher: Are there any other ways to figure out for 10 floors?

Stacy: I counted around it ten times. (She demonstrates by holding a 10-floor tower, tapping the top 3 cubes, and counting.) I went 1, 2, 3 . . . 4, 5, 6 . . . 7, 8, 9 . . . all the way around ten times.

Teacher: Why ten times?

Stacy: Because I know there are 10 floors.

Stacy's strategy was very interesting. Although she was using a count-all strategy, she seemed to understand that she was counting 3 ten times. This was similar to that of Erin, another student I observed earlier. Erin had experimented with counting by threes (3, 6, 9, and so on). She did well up to 12, but then had to count on by ones. I wanted to see if we could connect Stacy's strategy of counting all with Erin's counting-by-three attempt. Erin is usually hesitant to share her strategies so I needed to prompt her.

Teacher: Erin, you did something interesting early on when you were figuring for ten floors. What did you do?

Erin: I counted by threes.

Teacher: Can you show us how you did that?

Erin, pointing to the different rows: Three, 6, 9, 12.

Teacher: What happened after you got to 12?

Erin: I had to use my fingers. (She demonstrates by pinching the next row and saying 13, 14, 15.)

Teacher: Is Erin's idea similar to one we've seen?

Stacy: Mine.

Teacher: How?

Stacy: She was counting by threes and so was I. Like when I went 1, 2, 3 . . . 4, 5, 6 . . . 7, 8, 9. She was saying 3, 6, 9. It's the same.

At this point, I moved the discussion along by asking a particular student who doubled the fifth floor to share his strategy.

Teacher: Steven, you had an interesting way of approaching the problem. Can you tell the class what you did?

Steven: I doubled 15 and got 30.

Kayla: I did too.

Teacher: That's right; you did too.

At this point, some students seemed to connect with Kayla and Steven's idea. I heard a few say, "Oh, yeah." This seemed to confirm my suspicion that many just didn't see it in the moment. However, there were some who seemed unsure of what Steven was saying.

Teacher: Can you explain why you did that? How did you know it would work?

Steven: Well, you have 15, and then 5 more is 15 more. So 15 plus 15 is 30.

Teacher: I know what you mean, but I'm wondering if you could explain it in more detail. What do you mean five more is 15?

Steven: If you have 5 floors, you get 15 [rooms]. So if you go to 10 floors, that's 5 more floors with the same number of rooms.

Kayla: Five plus 5 is 10. It's doubling (pointing to the column for number of floors).

Steven: Yeah, so you have to double the other side too. Fifteen plus 15.

Kayla: It's like you're adding the same thing. See? (She takes a 10-floor model and breaks it in half.) This is 5 floors (holding one half of the tower) and this is 5 more floors (holding the other half).

Teacher: How many rooms are in each?

Both: Fifteen.

There were some more nods of understanding and some looks of confusion. I didn't want to push it so early in the exploration, so I moved on. They will encounter this problem many times this week and have plenty of opportunities to work with that idea through repeated reasoning.

There was one other student who seemed eager to share her strategy.

Mary: And if you double the rooms for the sixth floor, you get the rooms for a tower that's 12 floors tall.

Total Number of Floors in the Tower	Total Number of Rooms in the Tower
1	3
2	6
3	9
4	12

Figure 8.5 Tower table

Teacher: How do you know?

Mary: It's like a pattern. If you double 1 floor, it's 6, and if you double 2 floors, it's 12. That's how it works. (She points to the table in Figure 8.5.)

Other students were connecting to this idea and getting excited.

Teacher: So what if we doubled 3 floors?

Many Students: Eighteen!

Teacher: Wow! It seems like you all discovered something. I'm wondering if we can come up with a rule for figuring out the total number of rooms using what you just discovered.

Kayla: You just double it!

Class: Yeah.

Steven: It's the doubling rule!

Teacher: I like that. It's catchy. But I'm wondering if simply saying, "Double it" would explain to someone what they need to do. Can we be more specific?

Kayla: If you know how many rooms there are on a floor, you can double it to find out how many rooms are on higher floors.

Mary: If you know how many rooms are on a floor and you double the number of floors . . .

Kayla: You double the number of rooms!

Teacher: I'm going to write this rule down, because it's worth exploring tomorrow. I'm impressed with all the thinking I saw today. Nice work, everyone. It's time to get ready for reading.

All I can say is wow! I was not expecting that last part at all, but it was the most powerful part of the session. I think all the hard work with repeated reasoning, modeling, and counting gave more kids a way into seeing the doubling strategies Steve, Kayla, and Mary shared. If we had started the discussion with Mary's doubling idea, it might have gone over many students' heads, but after more time with building, counting, and completing tables, more students were able to make sense of it. This repeated reasoning helped others see the regularity in the task. I can't wait to pick up where they left off when we revisit these ideas tomorrow. Although only a few students seem solid with this idea right now, the excitement of the class is palpable, and I think they'll eagerly explore this idea over the next few days.

The task Ms. Chan used for her students was effective for setting students up to look for and express regularity in repeated reasoning. In this case for every floor of a tower, there was a fixed set of rooms. As towers grew taller, there was a rule for how they grew. The first tower students worked with grew by three rooms each time a floor was added. Other towers grew by different amounts, depending on how many rooms were in the initial floor. As students built towers and created tables, they engaged in repeated reasoning. Many students had to construct all parts of the towers and calculate the total number of rooms as each new floor was added. Over time, students noticed the regularity in how towers grew and the relationships between the number of floors and the number of rooms.

Activities like these lend themselves very well to this work with MP8 because students can generate rules for any given situation based on their discoveries through repeated reasoning. A related activity from Investigations involves students charting how many triangles cover a given number of trapezoids using pattern blocks. This is similar to the tower that had a base of three, as it takes three triangles to cover one trapezoid. Through repeated reasoning, students will discover that the same relationships occur and they can create a rule for calculating the number of triangles for any given number of trapezoids.

When the information is presented in a table format, students can see that one column goes up by one amount and the other column goes up by another amount. Students notice these number patterns and are excited to call them out. However, it's also important for them to look horizontally at the table to see the relationship between the values. It gives students a stronger sense of what's happening with the numbers and can lead to some powerful strategies for working with these values. For example, a student might notice that in a tower that grows by two, the relationship between the total number of floors and the total number of rooms is double. When asked to give the total number of rooms for a tower that is twenty floors high, they can apply this understanding and double twenty to get forty.

Some students in Ms. Chan's class saw the relationship between values and noticed that if you have a tower that is five floors high with fifteen total rooms, the same tower built to ten floors will have twice as many rooms. These ideas come to the forefront when teachers explicitly ask students to consider the relationships between values and to question why these regularities exist.

Not everyone in Ms. Chan's class was at the same level of understanding as Kayla and Mary, but all of them were able to notice and express some regularity from the task. While some students were able to comment that the towers grew by a certain amount, others were able to express the regularity within the relationships between the number of floors and the number of towers.

Just like in Ms. Solomon's class, the activity Ms. Chan adapted had multiple entry points for the range of learners in her classroom. Every student benefited in his or her own way from the activity, and Ms. Chan made sure to include them all in the discussions at the end of both classes. Her decision to have the more advanced thinking discussed at the end allowed the class to see physical representations of the mathematics as students who constructed all ten floors shared their models and counting strategies. This conversation provided some rich context for the abstract thinking of students such as Steven, Kayla, and Mary. As a result, when Mary, Kayla, and Steven expressed regularity in the form of a doubling rule—double the number of floors gives you double the number of rooms—more students had access to this idea.

MP8 is engaging for young students, but it also requires a lot of time. Teachers need to revisit the same ideas often for students to sort through regularities they see and develop ways to express them and articulate their reasoning. The vignettes here provided an intimate view into the teachers' thinking as they reflected on this work with students. We saw some students connect with ideas quickly, whereas others struggled to make sense of them. Regardless, the teachers kept finding creative ways to engage students and allow them to experience the mathematics in new ways so they could begin to see and express regularity in their math work.

Our role as teachers is very important in making these ideas come to light. In every example in this chapter, the teachers could have made getting the correct answer the focus. In Ms. Chan's class, students could have found how many rooms were in the ten-floor towers any way they wanted and she could have moved on. In Ms. Solomon's class, students could have found a bunch of ways to make ten, and she could have moved on. But both teachers chose to linger and explore some regularities with their students, and the results were quite powerful.

Teachers control the pace of the classroom and can decide whether to stay with a particular idea. Opportunities to explore regularity will present themselves often in K–2 classrooms, and we need to decide when the time is right to spend some time digging more deeply into the ideas. You don't always have to make it a big, multiday exploration. Sometimes you can just wonder aloud about a pattern or regularity that arises or ask a student who notices something to share his or her idea with the class. When students respond, they are expressing the regularity.

Not every idea about regularity that surfaces can be addressed in the moment, so I would recommend creating a class chart titled "Math Ideas We're Curious About" and put some of these wonderings on it as they arise. Then you can direct kids who finish their work early to try exploring some of these ideas on their own. Their work will likely involve trying many different examples to see if the pattern or regularity exists or always works. This repeated reasoning will support the students' understanding of the ideas so when you decide to visit them formally with the class, students will be able to express the regularity more easily.

No matter how you choose to engage your students, it's important to remember that these ideas need to linger with primary-grade students. Don't feel you need to rush them to all be at the same place at the same time. Think about how Ms. Solomon revisited an idea periodically over the course of months. Even then, not every student reached the same level of understanding. It helps to remember that students will encounter these regularities time and time again as they progress through the grades. Any work you do to help them slow down and think about what's happening mathematically is enormously beneficial. As your students get older and more sophisticated, their mathematical thinking around these ideas will, too. In many ways we're laying that strong foundation from which all future mathematical ideas will be built.

CHAPTER 9

Putting It All Together

Have you ever traveled with someone who plans itineraries that are completely jam-packed? I find it very frustrating, because you end up being in such a rush to see everything that it feels like you really never get to "see" anything. When I began implementing the Standards for Mathematical Practice with my second graders, I saw elements of most MPs in all the work we did together, and it was tempting to try to emphasize each of them during my lessons. After a few attempts I realized that the MPs are kind of like vacation destinations and we teachers are the travel planners. I learned from experience that when we try to emphasize all of them at the same time, we only skim the surface and do not devote the amount of attention to them that each one deserves.

There are only eight practice standards that describe the ways in which students should engage with the mathematics—just eight. And these practices are developed throughout students' mathematical careers, from kindergarten to twelfth grade and beyond. Therefore, they need to be carefully cultivated over time so that as students' knowledge, understanding, and skills develop, their facility with the MPs continues to grow accordingly.

Throughout this book we explored the MPs in depth to get a clearer sense of what each one looks like in K–2 classrooms. The aim was to explore them in isolation so we could consider the essential elements of the standards and give each one the attention it deserves. However, as we know, the MPs do not occur in isolation. Any given mathematical task, exploration, or activity you implement is likely to have elements that elicit many, if not most, of the MPs simultaneously.

Sometimes in a lesson the MPs are loosely connected in supportive roles. For example, in Ms. Perch's vignette from Chapter 3, her students were constructing mathematical arguments about whether the triangular half of a square was the same size as the rectangular half. Although the emphasis of that particular lesson was on constructing viable arguments and critiquing the reasoning of others (MP3), we saw how students attended to precision (MP6) as they made their arguments and how they used tools (MP5) such as scissors and rulers to help prove their points. The tools and focus on precision helped make stronger arguments.

Other times the MPs are tightly dependent upon one another. In Chapter 7, I discussed how my second graders were exploring the structure (MP7) of odd and even numbers by considering what happens when we added two odd numbers. The foundation of this work was through their repeated reasoning (MP8) as they tested a bunch of examples of adding two odd numbers. From this repeated reasoning they discovered the underlying structure of odd numbers and then used that structure to prove their conjecture that adding two odd numbers results in an even answer. Without engaging in MP8 as they did, their work with MP7 would have been limited.

On some occasions, the MPs are the focal point of a task, lesson, or unit, and at other times they run in the background while the content standards take center stage. In Ms. Hildago's counting station activity from Chapter 2 where students had to count objects and compare the counts on a recording sheet, she designed a task to specifically support her students' work in decontextualizing a situation. In this case, the MP was the focal point of the lesson. But not every one of Ms. Hildago's counting activities is designed to emphasize MP2. At times she creates tasks that focus on providing students with experiences counting without considering any of the MPs. That doesn't mean students are not working on perseverance (MP1) or constructing an argument (MP3) to explain why their count is correct, but in these tasks, the MPs are not the focal point.

These examples help bring to light the complexity of our work with the Standards for Mathematical Practice. Unlike content standards that are always specifically targeted in lesson objectives, the MPs are more nuanced in their presence in our daily lessons. Any task may have up to four or five MPs present in varying degrees. Knowing which MPs a teacher should emphasize at any given time comes down to three considerations: the needs of her or his students, the teacher's own content and pedagogical knowledge, and the specific curriculum materials the teacher is using.

Teachers know their students best. They work with them on a daily basis and have the clearest sense of their strengths and the areas where they need support.

As you consider the eight MPs with regard to your own students' knowledge, understanding, and skills, there may be times when you will want to emphasize one over the other. If your students seem really keen on noticing regularity in their repeated reasoning with addition, perhaps it makes sense to do some exploring of the structure(s) of addition (MP7). Maybe you notice that your students struggle to stay with a difficult task, in which case you may decide to emphasize MP1 and have some conversations with your students on perseverance.

This leads to our second consideration, which is the mathematical knowledge and understandings of the teacher. When we work to build and deepen our own content knowledge, we strengthen our abilities to effectively work on the MPs with our students. We also develop better lenses through which to recognize moments when elements of the MPs are present and worth exploring. I'm reminded of a quote from a *FoxTrot* comic strip where the math-savvy character named Jason says, "The more math you learn, the more math you'll see" (Amend 1993). I could not agree more with his statement. I found that the more I learned about the Standards for Mathematical Practice, the more I was able to recognize when they surfaced in my classroom.

Each teacher featured in the vignettes credited strong professional learning experiences with helping them develop the knowledge and skills to effectively integrate the MPs into their lessons. Some of these teachers are part of professional learning communities that meet regularly to discuss mathematics and teaching. Others regularly attend professional development seminars and webinars to continue their learning. Some read professional math books, articles, and blogs. Others use Twitter as a way to connect to teachers, coaches, and other educators deeply invested in math teaching.

I hope this book gives you a clearer sense of each of the MPs in the primary grades, but the book alone cannot provide all that teachers need to effectively implement the Standards for Mathematical Practice in their classrooms. Regardless of your preferred format for professional learning, I strongly encourage you to continue to seek ways to deepen your mathematical content and pedagogical knowledge.

The final consideration when thinking about implementing these practices in your classroom is the curriculum materials you use. There is a wide range of materials available to teachers, and, depending on your school and/or district, you may have a lot of choices and decisions to make. Most materials, whether they are part of a published math program or resources downloaded from the web, will refer to the MPs and give you suggestions for how to work on them with your students. These suggestions are a good place to start if you are new to implementing the MPs with students. However, the more experience you have implementing the MPs with fidelity and the more mathematical knowledge you develop, the more you'll develop a critical eye to allow you to analyze how successfully published materials address the MPs.

As you work to try lessons and follow suggestions using your resources, reflect on what you've learned from this book about how these practices should unfold with primary students. You may find that the resources you use support this work and your students respond well to the experiences, or you may find that the resources do not provide the right kinds of supports to allow you to do this work well with your students.

We need to consider the needs and abilities of our students along with our own understanding of the mathematics and weigh those against what we're being asked to do in a lesson. When these components are aligned, we can proceed as planned and see what unfolds with our students. When there is misalignment, we have to adjust the materials based on the kinds of experiences we want our students to have.

For example, I was looking for some tasks to support students in constructing viable arguments and came across one that had students determine whether particular shapes were symmetrical. The symmetry was not always easy to determine, and there were lots of opportunities for students to have different viewpoints and arguments. However, the task as written asked only that students write their arguments on the worksheet and hand it in. I saw this as a huge missed opportunity, because having students share their arguments with each other and have open debate is at the crux of MP3. I decided to use the task, but to alter what we did with the sheets to get students talking and working together.

Teachers have a huge responsibility to make sure the MPs receive enough attention in math class and to ensure students have many meaningful opportunities to engage with them. Primary teachers are in an exciting position because they shape students' first experiences with mathematics and can make a big difference by creating classroom climates that support this thoughtful work. By implementing the MPs with fidelity, we can ensure that our young students get a strong foundation in the practices that will support them as they grow and develop through their years in the K–12 system.

The Standards for Mathematical Practice are critically important as young students become strong mathematical thinkers. There is a lot to unpack with each standard; the work is ongoing as we explore new tasks and experiences that help bring these ideas to life. We too need to be continual learners in mathematics. As you move forward with your implementation of the MPs, you will refine and deepen your understanding of them and of how young students make sense of these ideas.

When students engage in the MPs, they are doing the meaningful work of mathematics. They think and reason. They work to make sense of the math and persevere when they encounter challenges. They talk with each other about their thinking and learn to listen to the thinking of others. They develop strategic methods for using the wide array of tools available to them. They discover structures through repeated reasoning and learn to use mathematics to make sense of events in their world.

Enjoy these moments with your students and cherish the opportunities to learn alongside them, for this work is as engaging for us as it is for our students. Together you will create rich and meaningful classroom experiences that students will remember.

REFERENCES

Amend, B. 1993. *FoxTrot* (comic strip). Kansas City, MO: Universal Uclick.

Bastable, V. 2012. "Using Story Situations to Illustrate the Meaning of the Operations." *California Math Council ComMuniCator.* http://mathleadership. org/wp-content/uploads/2013/04/Using-Story-Situations-to-Illuminate-the-Meaning-of-the-Operations.pdf.

Boaler, J. 2013. "Ability and Mathematics: The Mindset Revolution That Is Reshaping Education." *Forum* 55 (1): 143–152.

Boaler, J., C. Williams, and A. Confer. 2015. "Fluency Without Fear: Research Evidence on the Best Ways to Learn Math Facts." YouCubed at Stanford University. https://bhi61nm2cr3mkdgk1dtaov18-wpengine.netdna-ssl.com/wp-content/uploads/2015/03/FluencyWithoutFear-2015.pdf.

Burns, M. 2015. "Why I Like Using Open Number Lines (Though I Don't Like the Name)." *Marilyn Burns Math Blog.* http://marilynburnsmathblog.com/wordpress/why-i-like-using-open-number-lines-though-i-dont-like-the-name/.

Carpenter, T., E. Fennema, and M. Fanke. 1996. "Cognitively Guided Instruction: A Knowledge Base for Reform in Primary Mathematics Instruction." *The Elementary School Journal* 97 (1): 3–20.

Carpenter, T. P., and L. Levi. 2000. "Developing Conceptions of Algebraic Reasoning in the Primary Grades." Research Report.

Clements, D. 2007. "Early Childhood Mathematics Learning." In *Second Handbook of Research on Mathematics Teaching and Learning,* ed. F. K. Lester, Jr. New York: Information Age.

Clements, D. H., and J. Sarama. 2014. *Learning and Teaching Early Math: The Learning Trajectories Approach.* New York: Routledge.

Clements, D., J. Sarama, and A. M. DiBiase. 2003. *Engaging Young Children in Mathematics: Standards for Early Childhood Mathematics Education.* New York: Routledge.

Cogan, L., W. Schmidt, and R. Houang. 2013. "Implementing the Common Core State Standards for Mathematics: What We Know About Teachers of Mathematics in 41 States." Working Paper 33, Education Policy Center, Michigan State University, East Lansing.

Hill, H. C., and S. T. Lubienski. 2007. "Teachers' Mathematics Knowledge for Teaching and School Context: A Study of California Teachers." *Educational Policy* 21 (5): 747–768.

Hill, H. C., B. Rowan, and D. Loewenberg Ball. 2005. "Effects of Teachers' Mathematical Knowledge for Teaching on Student Achievement." *American Educational Research Journal* 42 (2): 371–406.

Hogan, M., and S. Alejandre. 2010. "Problem Solving—It Has to Begin with Noticing and Wondering." *California Math Council ComMuniCator.* http://mathforum.org/articles/communicator2010.html.

Illustrative Mathematics. 2014. Standards for Mathematical Practice: Commentary and Elaborations for K–5. Tucson, AZ: Author. http://commoncoretools.me/wp-content/uploads/2014/02/Elaborations.pdf.

Kazemi, E., and A. Hintz. 2014. *Intentional Talk: How to Structure and Lead Productive Mathematical Discussions.* Portland, ME: Stenhouse.

Ma, L. 2010. *Knowing and Teaching Elementary Mathematics.* New York: Taylor and Francis Routledge.

McCallum, B. 2011. *Structuring the Mathematical Practices.* http://commoncoretools.me/wp-content/uploads/2011/03/practices.pdf.

McCallum, W. 2015. "The Common Core State Standards in Mathematics." In *Selected Regular Lectures from the 12th International Congress on Mathematical Education.* Cham, Switzerland: Springer International.

National Council of Teachers of Mathematics. 2000. *Principles and Standards for School Mathematics.* Reston, VA: NCTM.

————. 2006. *Curriculum Focal Points for Prekindergarten Through Grade 8 Mathematics: A Quest for Coherence*. Reston, VA: NCTM.

National Governors Association Center for Best Practices, Council of Chief State School Officers. 2010. Common Core State Standards for Mathematics. Washington, DC: NGO/CCSSO.

Olson, T. A., M. Olson, and S. Capen. 2013. "Perceptions of the Standards for Mathematical Practice and Plans for Implementation." Proceedings of the 40th Annual Meeting of the Research Council on Mathematics Learning. Tulsa, Oklahoma, February.

Russell, S. J., D. Schifter, and V. Bastable. 2011. *Connecting Arithmetic to Algebra*. Portsmouth, NH: Heinemann.

Russell, S. J., D. Schifter, R. Kassman, V. Bastable, and T. Higgins. 2017. *Mathematical Argument in the Elementary Classroom*. Portsmouth, NH: Heinemann.

Sarama, J., and D. Clements. 2009. *Early Childhood Mathematics Education Research: Learning Trajectories for Young Children*. New York: Routledge.

Stein, C. 2007. "Let's Talk: Promoting Mathematical Discourse in the Classroom." *Mathematics Teacher* 101 (4): 285–289.

Sullivan, P., R. Zevenbergen, and J. Mousley. 2003. "The Contexts of Mathematics Tasks and the Context of the Classroom: Are We Including All Students?" *Mathematics Education Research Journal* 15 (2): 107–121.

TERC. 2016. *Investigations in Number, Data, and Space: K–5 Mathematics Curriculum*. Glenview, IL: Pearson.

Vaisenstein, A. 2006. "A Look at a Child's Understanding of Mathematical Ideas Through His Representations." In *Teachers Engaged in Research: Inquiry into Mathematics Classrooms, Grades Pre–K–2*, ed. S. Z. Smith and M. E. Smith. Greenwich, CT: Information Age.

Van de Walle, J. A., H. Lovin, and J. Bay-Williams. 2013. *Teaching Student-Centered Mathematics: Pearson New International Edition: Developmentally Appropriate Instruction for Grades Pre–K–2*. Vol. 1. Glenview, IL: Pearson Higher Ed.

Van de Walle, J. A., and S. Folk. 2005. *Elementary and Middle School Mathematics: Teaching Developmentally*. Toronto: Pearson Education Canada.

Wu, S., and F. Lin. 2016. "Inquiry-Based Mathematics Curriculum Design for Young Children—Teaching Experiment and Reflection." *Eurasia Journal of Mathematics, Science, & Technology Education* 12 (4): 843–860.

Zimba, J. 2014. "The Development and Design of the Common Core State Standards for Mathematics." *New England Journal of Public Policy* 26 (1): Article 10. http://scholarworks.umb.edu/nejpp/vol26/iss1/10.

INDEX

Page numbers followed by *f* indicate figures.